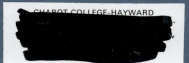

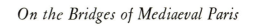

On the Bridges of Mediaeval Paris

"Esse Parisius est esse simpliciter"
"To be in Paris, is to be"

[From a letter written in 1323 to Jean de Jandun]

On the Bridges of

A Record of Early Fourteenth-Century Life

Virginia Wylie Egbert

Mediaeval Paris

Princeton University Press, New Jersey

COPYRIGHT © 1974 BY PRINCETON UNIVERSITY PRESS
PUBLISHED BY PRINCETON UNIVERSITY PRESS, PRINCETON AND LONDON
ALL RIGHTS RESERVED
LIBRARY OF CONGRESS CATALOGING IN PUBLICATION DATA WILL
BE FOUND ON THE LAST PRINTED PAGE OF THIS BOOK
THIS BOOK HAS BEEN COMPOSED IN LINOTYPE GRANJON
AND DESIGNED BY BRUCE CAMPBELL
PRINTED IN THE UNITED STATES OF AMERICA
COMPOSITION BY PRINCETON UNIVERSITY PRESS, PRINCETON, NEW JERSEY
PRINTED BY THE MERIDEN GRAVURE COMPANY, MERIDEN, CONNECTICUT

To the Memory of Donald Drew Egbert

Contents

Preface

The illuminated manuscript of the *Life of St. Denis*, MS fr. 2090-2092 in the Bibliothèque Nationale in Paris, has as great appeal today as it had in the Middle Ages when it was a treasured volume in the French royal library.

The manuscript was studied by Léopold Delisle in 1865 and was the subject of a monograph, *Légende de Saint Denis*, by Henry Martin in 1908. However, Martin's book, now out of print, gives only brief descriptions of the most interesting and original parts of the manuscript, the scenes on the Paris bridges, with little indication of their actual relation to contemporary Parisian life. This book makes no attempt to discuss the iconography of the life of St. Denis but rather presents a reexamination of these bridge scenes. By using mediaeval writings and documents I have tried to determine how realistic the pictures of everyday life are, and in what respects they are not so realistic as generally assumed. Literary sources add another dimension to the miniatures, and the combination gives a better conception of mediaeval life than either can do separately.

The introduction describes the manuscript and its history and discusses briefly the style of the miniatures in relation to a small group of other manuscripts.

Virginia Wylie Egbert
Princeton University

Acknowledgments

In the course of my work on this book I have received help from many people. I am especially grateful to François Avril, Rosalie Green, the late Dorothy Miner, and Carl Nordenfalk. I should also like to thank my colleagues at the Index of Christian Art, Isa Ragusa, Adelaide Bennett, and Elizabeth Menzies, Marcel Thomas and his staff at the Bibliothèque Nationale, Frederica Oldach and the staff of the Princeton University Library, Elizabeth Beatson, the late Robert Branner, François Bucher, Bruce Campbell, David Cowen, Margot Cutter, Michel Fleury, Alfred Foulet, Donald Griffin, Arthur Hanson, Mary Laing, Jacques Meurgey de Tupigny, John Peckham, Elizabeth Roth and Joseph Rankin of the New York Public Library, William F. Shellman, Jr., and Joseph Strayer. As always the files of the Index of Christian Art have been useful. Grants from the Spears Fund of the Department of Art and Archaeology, Princeton University, made it possible for me to work at the Bibliothèque Nationale and to buy most of the photographs.

The dedication of this book is an inadequate acknowledgment of the encouragement, advice, and help always given me by my late husband, Donald Egbert, whose joy in scholarship was contagious.

V. W. E.

List of Illustrations

Unless otherwise noted, photographs have been supplied by the institutions which own the manuscripts and are reproduced with the owner's permission.

On the Bridges of Mediaeval Paris

1. The presentation of the *Life of St. Denis* to King Philippe. *Life of St. Denis*, Paris, Bibliothèque Nationale, MS fr. 2090-2092, I, fol. 4 vo.

Introduction

When Philippe V was crowned king of France in 1317, he received from his chaplain Gilles, Abbot of Saint-Denis, the beautiful illuminated manuscript of the *Life of St. Denis*, now a prized possession of the Bibliothèque Nationale (MS fr. 2090-2092). The presentation scene is portrayed in the first miniature (fig. 1). A court official introduces the two kneeling figures of a monk, possibly the author, and Abbot Gilles who gives the book to the king.[1]

The dedication makes it clear that the Philippe who received the book bore the same name as his father for whom the manuscript was intended but who died before it was completed.[2] To Léopold Delisle belongs the credit for identifying the king as Philippe V and the abbot as Gilles de Pontoise, as well as for ascertaining the date 1317 when the manuscript was finished.[3]

Although the author's name is not mentioned, a later manuscript (MS lat. 5286 in the Bibliothèque Nationale), possibly copied from this one states that Abbot Gilles commissioned a monk of Saint-Denis, named Yves, to write a life of the monastery's patron saint.[4] The text identifies St. Denis with Dionysius the Areopagite whom Apostle Paul, on his visit to Athens, had converted to Christianity. By the middle of the ninth century, legend had combined into one saint three men living in three different periods: the first-century Dionysius the Areopagite, Denis the first bishop of Paris in the third century, and a fifth-century author of certain mystical writings. Trinitarian in subject and in construction, the *Life* honors the Trinity as well as St. Denis and his two companions Rusticus and Eleutherius, and it is divided into three parts, St. Denis' life from his birth to the arrival of Paul in Athens, the saint's acts from his conversion to his death, and a history of France with special relation to the cult of St. Denis.

The text was composed in Latin with a French translation by one Boitbien, interpolated in sections. It has been suggested that Philippe V was not so well educated as his father Philippe le Bel, who was described as "sufficienter litteris eruditus,"[5] and for this reason a French translation was added. But Philippe V's interest in vernacular literature may rather have motivated Boitbien's translation. Before he became king, Philippe surrounded himself with Provençal poets as members of his household staff; he himself is said to have written verses in French. His wife, Jeanne de Bourgogne, apparently shared this interest for she commissioned Philippe de Vitry's rhymed French translation of the moralized *Metamorphoses* of Ovid.

This copy of the *Life of St. Denis* remained in the possession of the kings of France until the early fifteenth century. A catalogue of the royal library in the Louvre, made in 1373 by Gilles Malet, refers to "The life of St. Denis and the lives of forty-six other saints, well illustrated, with an outer cover of material."[6] An entry in Jean le Bègue's inventory of 1411 reads as follows: "Item, the life of St. Denis and the lives of forty-six other saints, well illustrated, in an outer cover made of material with a 'tail,' written in a formal script, in French and Latin, beginning on fol. 2 *nobis ut mundi*, and on the last folio *donnant aux royaulx*; with two silver-gilt clasps."[7] In accordance with mediaeval practice in making inventories of manuscripts, the first words on the second page and those on the last page are recorded. The words in the 1411 inventory correspond with those on I, fol. 2 ro. and on the final page of III, fol. 111 ro. of MS fr. 2090-2092, establishing without a doubt the identity of this manuscript with the one in the king's library. Furthermore, it clearly indicates that the third part of the text was already missing. At the end of his second inventory, begun in 1413, Jean le Bègue lists fifty-five manuscripts, including the *Life of St. Denis*, which had been removed from the royal library in 1414 or 1415.[8] No reason was given for their removal. We know, however, that books were continually borrowed from the library in the Louvre and were often given as presents to royalty.

Sometime during the fifteenth century this manuscript came into the possession of Jeanne de Laval, the second wife of René d'Anjou. Her arms appear on the first folio (fig. 2), and an escutcheon bearing the lion passant of Laval was painted on the last page (fig. 3).[9] The book may have been inherited by Jeanne, a great granddaughter of Charles VI, or it may have been a gift from René who, in turn, may have received it from a member of the royal family to which he was closely connected by the marriage in 1413 of his sister to Charles VII. When René died his library, which had been moved to Aix, passed to his nephew and heir, Charles d'Anjou, who at his death is. said to have left the books to the Dominican monastery of Saint-Maximin-de-Provence.[10] In her will Jeanne gave all her books to the chapter of St. Tugal of Laval for the use of the daughters of the comtes de Laval as long as they lived in that town.[11] The *Life of St. Denis*, therefore, was probably among the books bequeathed either to Charles d'Anjou or to the chapter of St. Tugal. No trace of it is known for another two hundred years, until 1662, when it was returned to the royal library in the collection of books, paintings, and statues presented by Hippolyte, comte de Bethune, to

2. Arms of Jeanne de Laval. *Life of St. Denis*, Paris, Bibliothèque Nationale, MS fr. 2090-2092, I, fol. 1 ro.

Louis XIV.[12] The arms inscribed on the binding are those of the comte de Bethune who probably divided the manuscript into the present three volumes.

The third part of the *Life of St. Denis*, missing from MS fr. 2090-2092, is found in a fragmentary

3. Arms of Laval. *Life of St. Denis*, Paris, Bibliothèque Nationale, MS fr. 2090-2092, III, fol. 111 vo.

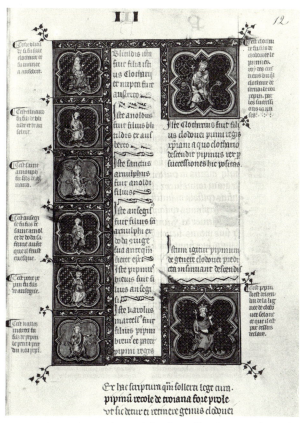

4. Genealogy of French royal family. *Life of St. Denis*, Paris, Bibliothèque Nationale, MS lat. 13836, fol. 12 ro.

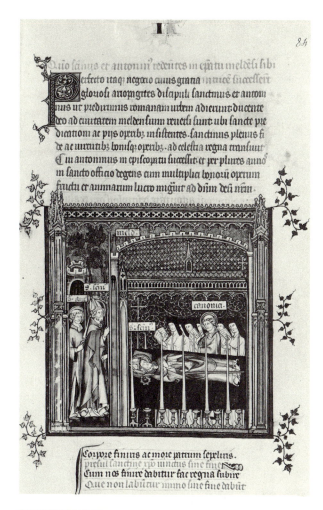

5. The death of St. Sanctinus. *Life of St. Denis*, Paris, Bibliothèque Nationale, MS fr. 2090-2092, III, fol. 84 ro.

6. The death of Simon de Bucy. *Le Grand Obituaire de Notre Dame de Paris,* Paris, Bibliothèque Nationale, MS lat. 5185 CC, fol. 224 ro.

manuscript in the Bibliothèque Nationale, MS lat. 13836.[13] Its late fifteenth- or early sixteenth-century binding seems to indicate that it was incomplete at that period. The manuscript formed part of the Coislin (olim Séguier) library which was given by Henri du Cambout, duc de Coislin and bishop of Metz, in 1732 to the monastery of Saint-Germain-des-Prés (MS 1082);[14] it was transferred to the Bibliothèque Nationale in late 1795 or early 1796.

The script of this manuscript is the same as that of MS fr. 2090-2092. The measurements of its pages (6⅜ x 9⅞ inches) are just about one half inch larger in length and width than those of MS fr. 2090-2092 whose margins have obviously been cut,[15] but the measurements of the actual text (3¾ x 5¾ inches) are generally the same. The appearance of the pages, however, is quite different because in MS lat. 13836 a French translation has been added in the margins giving a crowded impression (figs. 4, 5). The manuscript bears the signature of the scribe Guillaume l'Escot, the date 1317 when it was completed, and the name of Philippe V to whom it was presented.[16]

The similarities in figure style, architectural detail, background ornament and pen flourishes reveal a common workshop for these two manuscripts of the *Life of St. Denis* (figs. 1, 7, 8, 17). MS lat. 13836 is decorated with seventy-four small figures of kings and queens, ranging in size from ½ to 1⅓ inches, and displaying an amazing variety of types. Some of these may be attributed to the artist of the bridge scenes in MS fr. 2090-2092 (figs. 9, 10). The majority, however, were executed by another illuminator whose style is characterized by more linear drapery and the indication of the lower eyelid (fig. 11).

Opinions differ on the relationship between MSS lat.

7. St. Denis appears to Hermit John. The soul of King Dagobert saved from devils through the intercession of Hermit John. *Life of St. Denis*, Paris, Bibliothèque Nationale, MS lat. 13836, fol. 1 ro.

8. Imprisonment of St. Denis. *Life of St. Denis*, Paris, Bibliothèque Nationale, MS fr. 2090-2092, III, fol. 32 ro.

9. Detail of fig. 4

10. On the bridges of Paris. *Life of St. Denis*, Paris, Bibliothèque Nationale, MS fr. 2090-2092, I, fol. 4 vo. (detail)

13836 and fr. 2090-2092.[17] I am convinced that they originally formed one manuscript. Work on the manuscript seems to have been interrupted between the second and third parts. At the end of the second part the colophon, ". . . Ici fenit ces verz boitbien" records the completion of the French translation by Boitbien.[18] He apparently did not continue to translate the third part. Another translator and another artist joined the group working on this project. The subject of the third part could form an entity; this last section of the *Life of St. Denis*, therefore, may have been bound originally as a separate volume which could easily have become separated from the first one.

A more complete text of the *Life of St. Denis* is found in MS lat. 5286 in the Bibliothèque Nationale. Its illustrations were probably executed before the middle of the fourteenth century.[19] Although they are almost exact copies of all the miniatures of MS fr. 2090-2092, the ink drawings produce a somber effect and the manuscript lacks the charm and richness of the painted, presentation book (fig. 12). MS lat. 5286 contains a full-page Crucifixion miniature and another depicting St. Denis' ecclesiastic hierarchy, neither of which is found in MS fr. 2090-2092, as well as slight differences

in the bridge scenes of Paris; it also includes several full-page drawings lacking in MS lat. 13836. The illuminator of MS lat. 5286 may have copied directly

11. Charlemagne. *Life of St. Denis*, Paris, Bibliothèque Nationale, MS lat. 13836, fol. 34 vo.

12. The presentation of the *Life of St. Denis*, Paris, Bibliothèque Nationale, MS lat. 5286, fol. 1 ro.

13. Walled city of Carcassonne.

from MS fr. 2090-2092, adding a few scenes not found in his model, or he may possibly have copied another unknown manuscript of the *Life of St. Denis*.

The book (MS fr. 2090-2092) presented to Philippe V comprises three historiated initials and seventy-seven large miniatures, including thirty scenes on the bridges of Paris.

The miniatures are painted in light colors, predominantly pinks, blues, vermilion, greens, and gold which lend a festive quality to the whole work, even to the scenes of martyrdom. There is a variety of patterns: foliate, punched gold, and geometric forms inclosing fleur-de-lys, rosettes and swastikas decorate the backgrounds, and delicate branches of leaves extend from the frames into the margins.

Although the artists had little real understanding of architecture, nonetheless they seem to have made a deliberate attempt to represent architecture that was familiar to them. The city wall, depicted without perspective, is a typical mediaeval, crenelated wall similar to the one still visible at Carcassonne (figs. 8, 13), the doll-house like church with exterior and interior views

Urbem gallox subit urbem parisiorum
Non sens etatm · non gentilem tritate
Non penas ueritus hic pater emeritus

14. [*opposite*] Arrival of St. Denis in Paris. *Life of St. Denis*, Paris, Bibliothèque Nationale, MS fr. 2090-2092, II, fol. 97 ro.

15. The mediaeval palace of the Louvre. *Très Riches Heures du duc de Berry*, Chantilly, Musée Condé, fol. 10 vo. (detail)

16. South side of the choir of the cathedral of Notre Dame, Paris

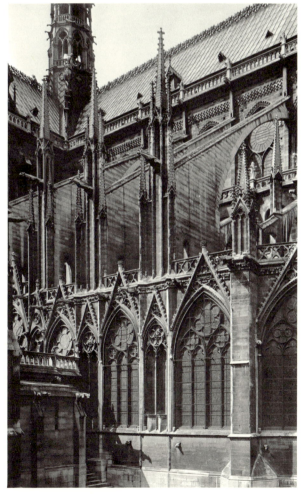

shown simultaneously, has a rose window, and the bridge towers are reminiscent of the thirteenth-century towers of the old palace of the Louvre (figs. 14, 15).[20] Enclosing the miniatures are architectural frames composed of piers surmounted by three crocketed pinnacles which may have been influenced by the piers on the south side of the choir of Notre Dame (figs. 14, 16).[21]

The figure style of the large miniatures is fairly consistent but slight differences, especially in the rendering of the faces, indicate the work of several artists in the same shop. The faces of Gilles de Pontoise and King Philippe (fig. 1) are more carefully modeled than any of the others and are drawn in a different brownish ink. A comparison of the face of the king in this scene with that of Philippe le Bel in MS lat. 13836 (fig. 17) suggests that the former portrait was perhaps meant to represent Philippe le Bel for whom the manuscript was originally intended. In contrast to the serene rather static figures of the large miniatures, the more animated small ones (about ½ inch high) on the bridges are drawn in a sketchier style, probably by a single artist.

The influence of the illuminator Honoré who was working on the Rue de Boutebrie, in the late thirteenth century, is evident in the figure style and in such characteristic details as the inverted V eyebrows,

17. Philippe le Bel. *Life of St. Denis*, Paris, Bibliothèque Nationale, MS lat. 13836, fol. 120 ro.

the marks on the cheeks, and the use of identifying inscriptions (figs. 18, 19).

Related to the *Life of St. Denis* is a manuscript of the Decretals of Gratian, MS lat. 3893 in the Bibliothèque Nationale. A colophon gives the name of the scribe Thomas de Wymonduswold, an Englishman working in Paris,[22] and the date 1314 when he completed this manuscript. A miniature showing Christ enthroned, presenting symbols of spiritual and temporal power to a St. Peter and a king, reveals certain similarities to MS fr. 2090-2092 in the drawing of the

18. The sinner and the hypocrite with corresponding personifications of Humility and Pride. *La Somme le Roi*, London, British Museum, MS Add. 54180, fol. 97 vo.

19. Saints Sanctinus and Antoninus journey to Rome. *Life of St. Denis*, Paris, Bibliothèque Nationale, MS fr. 2090-2092, III, fol. 80 ro.

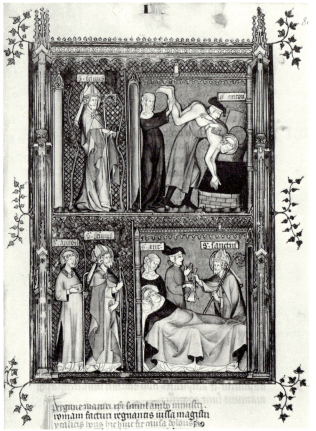

faces, the hair, the cheek marks, and in the ornament of the background and initials (figs. 20, 21). The other miniatures seem to have been executed by another artist. The colors in the two manuscripts are similar although those of the Decretals are a little darker, and a certain common iconographic vocabulary appears in the marginal figures of the Decretals and in the bridge scenes of the *Life of St. Denis*.[23]

Another manuscript in the Bibliothèque Nationale, *Le Grand Obituaire de Notre Dame de Paris*, MS lat. 5185 CC, contains a miniature reminiscent of MS fr.

20. Christ giving symbols of spiritual and temporal power. Decretals of Gratian, Paris, Bibliothèque Nationale, MS lat. 3893, fol. 1 ro.

21. The Trinity. *Life of St. Denis*, Paris, Bibliothèque Nationale, MS fr. 2090-2092, I, fol. 107 vo. (detail)

2090-2092.[24] In the death scene of Simon de Bucy (Bishop of Paris who died in 1304) the faces of the bishops, the colors and the background ornament show a kinship to the style of the *Life of St. Denis* (figs. 5, 6).

An exquisite small Bible, measuring only 4¾ x 7⅜ inches, MS lat. 248 in the Bibliothèque Nationale, was probably produced in the same workshop as the presentation copy of the *Life of St. Denis*. On the fly leaf of each of its volumes, Jean Flamel, the secretary of the duc de Berry, described the Bible as having belonged to Philippe le Bel and noted its present ownership by Jean duc de Berry, who proudly added his signature at the end of each volume. The light pastel colors of this manuscript are the same as those of MS fr. 2090-2092 and the figure style is similar (figs. 22, 23). Many comparable details may be found in the two manuscripts, similar foliate ornament, line end-

22. [*left*] Evangelist Mark. Bible of Philippe le Bel, Paris, Bibliothèque Nationale, MS lat. 248, II, fol. 258 vo.

23. St. Regulus celebrating Mass in Arles. *Life of St. Denis*, Paris, Bibliothèque Nationale, MS fr 2090-2092, III, fol. 67 ro.

ings, architectural frames and crockets, and similar drawing of the faces (except for the indication of the lower eyelid in ms lat. 248).

Two other manuscripts, a Gradual, ms lat. 1337 in the Bibliothèque Nationale, and a book of Hours, ms Spencer 56 in the New York Public Library,[25] were executed, I believe, by a less accomplished artist in the workshop which produced mss fr. 2090-2092, lat. 13836, and lat. 248. Here again the colors, background ornament, facial types, and figure style reveal a close family relationship (figs. 24-30).

Since the publication of ms Spencer 56 by Delisle in 1905, it has generally been assumed that the Hours were made about 1350 for Blanche duchesse d'Orléans.[26] The book includes prayers for Blanche, for Philippe, for the king, queens, and royal children. Delisle believed that these prayers indicated that the manuscript was probably executed between 1350 and

1360 for Blanche d'Orléans who married Philippe VI in 1344. The resemblance, however, between this manuscript, ms fr. 2090-2092, and the Bible of Philippe le Bel (ms lat. 248) makes an earlier date more probable. Then who was the Blanche for whom this book of Hours was intended? That she had royal connections seems evident from the placing of a prayer for herself immediately following those for the king and his family. Of the royal ladies named Blanche, living

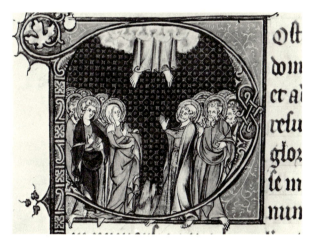

25. The Ascension. *Life of St. Denis*, Paris, Bibliothèque Nationale, ms fr. 2090-2092, I, fol. 20 vo.

26. The Virgin Mary with the Apostles in Jerusalem. Bible of Philippe le Bel, Paris, Bibliothèque Nationale, ms lat. 248, II, fol. 377 ro.

24. The Ascension. Gradual, Paris, Bibliothèque Nationale, ms lat. 1337, fol. 158 ro.

27. The Betrayal of Christ. Hours, New York Public Library, MS Spencer 56, fol. 229 ro.

28. The Trinity. Hours, New York Public Library, MS Spencer 56, fol. 133 ro.

at the beginning of the fourteenth century, Blanche de Bourgogne is a likely candidate.[27] Delisle assumed that the Philippe for whom the prayers were offered was the husband of Blanche. There is, however, no reference to this relationship in the text, only supplications for the safety and well-being of "your serv-

ant Philippe." Blanche de Bourgogne and her husband Charles, brother of Philippe V and comte de la Marche, had a son Philippe born in 1313.[28] A year later Blanche was imprisoned on the charge of adultery and finally, in 1322, was repudiated by her husband when he ascended the throne as Charles IV. Following

29. The Trinity. Bible of Philippe le Bel, Paris, Bibliothèque Nationale, MS lat. 248, I, fol. 462 ro.

30. The Death of the Virgin Mary. Gradual, Paris, Bibliothèque Nationale, MS lat. 1337, fol. 257 vo.

16

her imprisonment in 1314, all hopes for the future must have centered on her royal son, for whose safety it would have been only natural to pray. If indeed this book of Hours was made for Blanche de Bourgogne, it would have been executed between 1313 and 1321 during the brief life of her son and close in time to the *Life of St. Denis.*

It is interesting to speculate on the identity of the artist who illuminated this manuscript. We know that Blanche's parents, Otton IV de Bourgogne and Mahaut d'Artois, were patrons of the illuminator Maciot, to whom, in 1302, they gave a house in the Rue Simon-le-Franc.[29] This artist was still working at his profession in 1313 when his name appeared in the Paris tax register.[30] Blanche may well have given this commission to her parents' protégé or to one of his assistants. Maciot's name also appears in a 1313 list of the members of Philippe le Bel's household, and six years later he was the only illuminator mentioned in the estates of Philippe V.[31]

Unfortunately the illuminators of the *Life of St. Denis* did not record their names as did the scribe Guillaume l'Escot and the translator Boitbien. For this important commission an artist of distinction must have been chosen, one who enjoyed a prestige comparable to that held by Maciot in court circles. He is the only illuminator known to have been connected with all the people who originally owned MSS fr. 2090-2092, lat. 13836, lat. 248, and possibly Spencer 56, manuscripts apparently from the same workshop. It is tempting therefore to attribute these manuscripts, created for members of the French royal family, to Maciot and his assistants.[32] The workshop which produced the *Life of St. Denis* while carrying on the tradition of Honoré revitalized it with new elements. Its influence on Parisian illumination continued in the following decade, in works associated with Pucelle (figs. 31, 32).[33]

31. The Crucified Christ. *Life of St. Denis*, Paris, Bibliothèque Nationale, MS fr. 2090-2092, I, fol. 34 ro. (detail)

32. The Crucifixion. Hours of Jeanne d'Evreux (54.1.2), fol. 68 vo., New York, Metropolitan Museum of Art, the Cloisters

Scenes on the Bridges of Paris from MS fr. 2090-2092

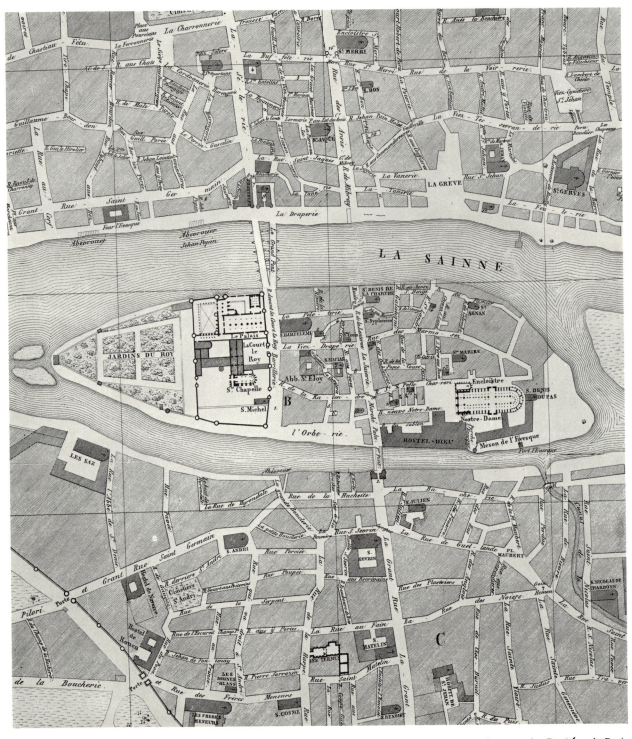

33. Map of Paris in the early fourteenth century. Adapted by W. F. Shellman, Jr. from A. Lenoir's map in P. Géraud, *Paris sous Philippe-le-Bel*, Paris, 1837

Paris, the site of St. Denis' major ministry as well as the capital of the French king, occupies a prominent place in the *Life of St. Denis* (MS fr. 2090-2092). The illuminators of this manuscript, having depicted Rome and Arles by almost identical architectural formulas, portrayed Paris in a completely different way, by a series of animated scenes on the bridges leading to the heart of the city. The Paris revealed here is the city of ordinary people engaged in their daily occupations and amusements. Aristocrats and clergy are conspicuously absent, a reflection perhaps on the tensions between them and Philippe le Bel, for whom the manuscript was begun. In this gift for the king, donor and illuminators have commemorated Paris, whose importance had been recognized years before by Louis IX as a support to the king against his peers and barons as well as against foreigners.[34]

Any visitor to mediaeval Paris would have soon discovered that the peak of its activity centered on the two bridges connecting the island of the Cité with the Right and Left Banks. The Grand Pont, spanning the northern branch of the Seine, led to the Right Bank; further east on the south, the Petit Pont extended from the Rue de Marché Palu of the Cité to the Grande Rue or the Rue St. Jacques on the Left Bank (fig. 33).

Bridges over the Seine dated back to Roman times. Sometimes of wood, sometimes of stone, they were rebuilt again and again in the course of centuries after being damaged by fire and flood.

One of these devastating floods raged through Paris on December 21, 1296. An eyewitness, a monk of the college of St. Bernard, described the catastrophe. "In the year 1296 Paris was so inundated by water from continual rain, ice and snow that the Petit Pont and a large part of the adjoining Petit Châtelet collapsed on the feast of Apostle Thomas; besides, the Grand Pont with all its houses, up to the one nearest the church of St. Lefredius, was terribly shaken and its very foundations exposed. . . ." The Seine did not subside until March 25th. A ferry service was established while the stone bridges were being replaced by wooden ones. The reconstruction of the Petit Pont took a month; "wooden bridges were made, the first people crossed the Petit Pont in April 1297." But work on the Grand Pont continued for seven months; "people crossed the Grand Pont first on November 12, 1297."[35]

The wooden bridge replacing the Grand Pont was located to the east of the old site and connected the Rue St. Barthélemy (on the Cité) with the Rue Vielle Joaillerie (on the Right Bank).[36] Later in the fifteenth century this bridge came to be known as the Pont-aux-Changeurs. After the flood of 1296 the mills which had been moored under the Grand Pont were gradually reconstructed on the ruins of its piers. A chain of wooden buildings was erected, connected by a narrow passageway which formed an acute angle with the Grand Pont; this was the origin of the Pont-aux-Meuniers, first mentioned in 1323 (fig. 33).[37]

Throughout the *Life of St. Denis* the bridges are depicted as monumental stone structures (fig. 1). We know, however, from the account of the flood of 1296, quoted above, that the stone bridges destroyed in that year were replaced by wooden ones. The fourteenth-century artist was either modeling his pictures on an earlier unknown manuscript or was portraying, from memory, the more splendid preflood bridges. Each bridge probably had two gates, one at the Cité entrance, the other on the mainland.[38] Here the scenes showing the Cité, carefully inscribed *Parisius*, have been telescoped so that the Grand Pont, with four, five, or six arches, and the Petit Pont, usually with only two arches, are represented on the same plane and converge on gates opening into the walled city. The bridge towers were undoubtedly covered to protect the watchmen from rain and snow. These superstructures may have looked like the ones depicted in this manuscript or perhaps like those shown in the Hours of Jeanne d'Evreux (fig. 34). Unlike the bridges in the *Life of St. Denis*, the Grand Pont had one arch wider than the others through which boats passed. Such an arch existed in the wooden bridge of 1297.[39] The il-

34. St. Louis' prayer book miraculously returned to him in prison. Hours of Jeanne d'Evreux (54.1.2), New York, Metropolitan Museum of Art, the Cloisters, fol. 154 vo.

luminator tried to indicate abutments against the piers but he obviously did not understand architecture for he has shown corbeled arches which could not have been used for such spans or supported such weight.

The Grand Pont was the domain of the money changers and the goldsmiths. In 1304 Philippe le Bel ordained that the Exchange should be on the east side of the bridge, and he prohibited the money changers from doing business elsewhere.[40] The forges were on the opposite side of the bridge. Some of the locations of the money changers and the goldsmiths were held for life as grants from the king until Philippe V in 1320 retracted these arrangements and sold the concessions at auction.[41] According to the 1313 tax register, a number of drapers also had their shops on this bridge.[42]

In the twelfth century, philosophers known as Parvi-Pontins lived on the Petit Pont;[43] later they were succeeded by merchants. Here tolls were collected on food supplies and merchandise brought into the city by land. This bridge became such a bustling center of trade that Joinville, in describing the burning of the bazaar at Damietta by the Turks in 1249, wrote, "The damage that followed from this was as great as if—which God forbid!—someone were, tomorrow, to set fire to the Petit-Pont in Paris."[44]

The Seine linked Paris with the outside world. Ships were constantly arriving, bringing "the riches of all parts of the world . . . wines of Greece, of Grenache, of La Rochelle, of Gascogne, of Burgundy . . . [and] quantities of wheat, rye, peas, beans, hay, charcoal and wood."[45]

The river was a favorite resort of University students. The majority were evidently more carefree than studious since Robert de Sorbonne felt the need to warn that "The scholar walking on the banks of the Seine in the evening ought not to indulge in sports but rather think about his lesson and repeat it."[46] Here, too, men were always fishing for pleasure and for livelihood. In warm weather there were boating parties and swimmers refreshing "their bodies burned by the heat of summer."[47]

This is the Paris we find so vividly depicted in the *Life of St. Denis.*

On the Seine a man paddles a boat past the bridges of Paris where two young men, in animated conversation, are approaching the raised portcullis of the fortified gate at the end of the Grand Pont. From the opposite direction a youth saunters along the Petit Pont, leading a monkey on a leash. Monkeys were such popular pets in the Middle Ages that they are specifically mentioned in toll regulations: "A merchant owes four deniers if he intends to sell his monkeys, but if they belong to someone who has bought them for his own amusement no toll is charged. When monkeys perform before the toll guard, their keeper and everything he buys goes free as does a jongleur for a snatch of song."[48] This engaging custom of granting free passage to the owner of a performing monkey gave rise to the expression, "payer en monnoie de singe."

The later manuscript of the *Life of St. Denis* (MS lat. 5286, fol. 1 ro. in the Bibliothèque Nationale) shows a slight variation on this scene with the horsemen replaced by two men shoeing a horse (fig. 35).

35. *Life of St. Denis*, MS lat. 5286, Paris, Bibliothèque Nationale, fol. 1 ro. (detail of fig. 12)

Plate I. 1, fol. 4 vo. (detail)

St. Denis' arrival in Paris is the principal episode of this miniature (fig. 14). Although, according to legend, the saint came from Arles and therefore must have approached the Cité from the Petit Pont, he and his companions are shown crossing the Grand Pont.[49] On the smaller bridge a tonsured cleric directs a man laying a cobblestone road. The practice of paving streets in Paris dated back to an order of Philippe Auguste in 1184. The chronicler Rigord reports: "When he [Philippe Auguste] approached the palace windows from which, for entertainment, he used to look out at the Seine, the horse-drawn wagons crossing the Cité raised such a fetid smell from mud piled in the streets that the king could endure it no longer. He decided that it was necessary to put into effect a project already considered by some of his predecessors but never executed because of the great expense. Having assembled the leaders of the city and the provost he gave the order to pave the main streets with big stones."[50] Two men, "paveurs," employed for such work are mentioned in the tax register of 1313.[51]

Fishing on the Seine was regulated by the king, the canons of Notre-Dame, and the abbey of Saint-Germain-des-Prés. Three year contracts were granted to fishermen who had to swear on the Bible that they wouldn't take carp, pike, or eels under a certain size.[52] Here two fishermen, leaning from their boats, pull in a net of good-sized fish.

Plate II. 11, fol. 97 ro. (detail)

The bridges of mediaeval Paris reverberated with a confusion of sounds. One might have heard the clear, high voices of a group of clerics singing on the river, intermingled with shouts from the watchman on a gate, the clatter of horses' hooves, and hammering on an anvil.

Money changers and goldsmiths, as we noted earlier, had long been established on the Grand Pont. Two of them are depicted here in their shops. Jean de Jandun tells us that "there are excellent fashioners of metal vases, chiefly of gold and silver, pewter and copper, to be found on the Grand Pont and their hammers on the anvils resound in a harmonious cadence."[53]

From the wall of the bridge gate a watchman directs a young horseman followed by an attendant on foot. Although it seems odd that the young man should be carrying his falcon into the congested city, this is exactly what a Parisian householder advised: "At this stage of training your hawk, you must keep him on your wrist more than ever before, taking him to law-courts and among people gathered in church or elsewhere, and into the streets. Keep him with you as long as you can, day and night; and sometimes perch him in streets, that he may see and accustom himself to men, horses, carts, hounds, and everything else."[54]

On the Petit Pont a porter, staggering under a heavy sack slung over his shoulder, approaches a shop displaying wallets and knives where a customer bargains with a woman shopkeeper for the knife he has chosen.

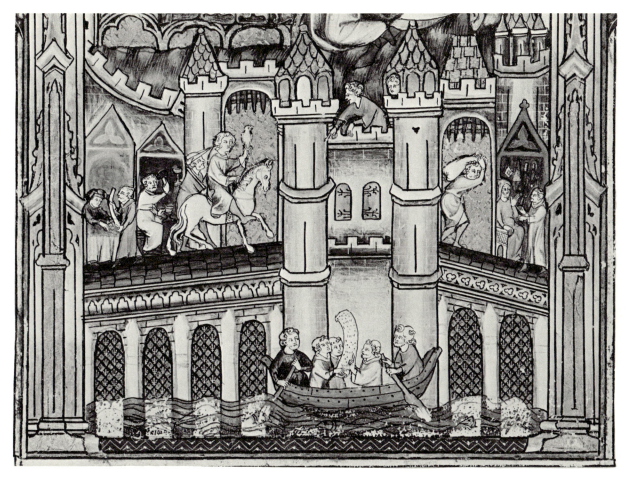

Plate III. 11, fol. 99 ro. (detail)

A muleteer prods his laden beast past the shops of the money changer and the goldsmith on the Grand Pont while from a boat on the river a man attempts to spear a fish.

Plate IV. II, fol. 105 vo. (detail)

From the tower of the gate at the end of the Grand Pont a guard scrutinizes the porter pushing a wheelbarrow, loaded with bales, past the money changer and the goldsmith in their customary places.

On the Petit Pont a beggar, carrying a baby on his back, and leaning on a staff, receives alms from a woman cutler seated in a doorway where her knives are hanging. Guillaume de Villeneuve, writing at the end of the thirteenth century, complained of his own miserable poverty: "I have pawned the little I had, so that poverty lords it over me. And then I had to pawn my very clothes, frequenting taverns has disrobed me. I don't know what will become of me or where to go." With sympathy he must have observed "The streets cluttered with poor people and at every step one hears, 'Beggar! God, who calls me? Come here and empty this bowl.'"[55]

All cargoes arriving in Paris by ship were subject to tolls at the main arch of the Grand Pont. In this scene a shipmaster, standing on a cargo of wine casks, sculls his ship, towed by a small boat of the kind that always guided the larger ships toward the toll station.

Plate V. ii, fol. iii ro. (detail)

Crossing the Grand Pont at a brisk trot, two horsemen, one mounted sidesaddle, are accompanied by an attendant on foot. A ragpicker, equipped with a basket and stick, enters the gate to the Cité from the Petit Pont where a woman is spinning in the doorway of her house or shop.

On the Seine a man fishes from a boat paddled by his companion.

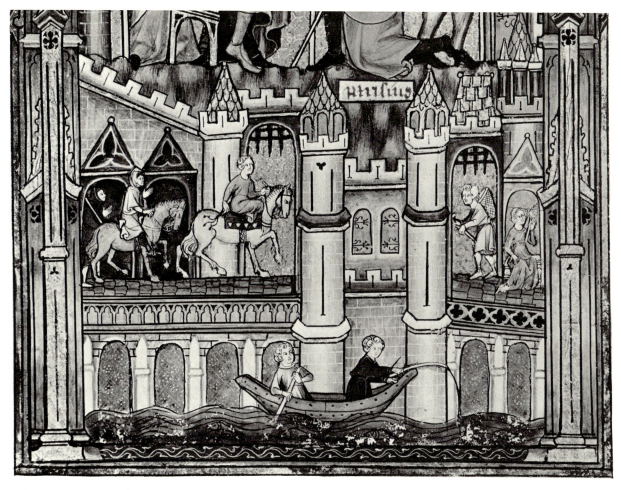

Plate VI. II, fol. 115 ro. (detail)

A group of travelers arrive at a gate of the Cité. Five passengers are seated in a single row in a coach driven by a postilion mounted on one of two horses pulling in tandem. The traces fastened directly against the sides of the coach indicate a narrow vehicle, the only kind that could have squeezed through the narrow mediaeval streets.

In a doorway at the far end of the Petit Pont a woman consults a doctor. Jean de Jandun reports that in the streets of Paris there were so many physicians, dressed in their characteristic hats and rich garments going on their rounds, that anyone who needed a doctor could easily find one.[56] Here the doctor while examining a urinal reaches for his fee. Some people complained that ". . . physicians . . . sell knowledge for pennies; . . . They find gain so sweet and pleasant that the physician wishes he had sixty patients for the one he has, . . . indeed two hundred or two thousand, so much covetousness and guile burn in their hearts."[57] This criticism, however, was not shared by the patient who exclaimed, "O how esteemed are these eminent physicians!"[58]

All shipping coming into Paris was strictly regulated by the corporation of the *marchands de l'eau*. When a cargo of wine arrived, only a resident of Paris could unload it, but a foreign shipper was permitted to sell his wine *in* his boat.[59] Since cargoes were allowed to remain in ships only three days after arrival, it was necessary to sell quickly. A prospective buyer is shown seated among casks in a boat, sampling the newly arrived wine, while, in another boat, a Parisian pays for the cask he has chosen.

Plate VII. II, fol. 125 ro. (detail)

Cargo ships arriving in Paris were unloaded at the Place de la Grève situated on the Right Bank. There the ships were greeted by a noisy, milling crowd of customs officers, weighers, criers, porters, merchants, and curious bystanders.

In this miniature a shipmaster supervises the unloading of his cargo of wheat, which is protected by awnings. A man with a sack over his shoulder descends a gangplank from one of the two ships locked together by another gangplank. The scene is set before the Grand Pont although in reality La Grève was east of the bridge.

Plate VIII. II, fol. 127 ro. (detail)

Merchants dealing in pet birds and birds of chase did a thriving business in mediaeval Paris.[60] Here one of these merchants displays a charming goldfinch in a cage to two men, one of whom has already acquired a falcon.

Nearby, beside the open gate at the end of the Grand Pont, a leper, his face and hands spotted with disease, sits begging; he holds a bowl in one hand and in the other a clapper to warn passers-by to keep at a safe distance. According to legend, St. Martin was said to have healed a leper at the mainland gate of the Grand Pont.[61] A few years after this miniature was painted these unfortunate outcasts had disappeared from the Paris scene. In 1321 a fantastic rumor spread through France accusing lepers and Jews of conspiring to poison all the country's water supplies. Many Jews were banished and their property confiscated but, in a frenzy of fear, almost all lepers were imprisoned or killed.[62]

In a shop on the Petit Pont an apothecary holding a pestle in each hand grinds his preparations in a mortar.[63] Although members of this profession were scattered throughout the city, they were especially associated with this bridge: ". . . the apothecaries who prepare medicines and who blend an infinite variety of spices live on the celebrated Petit Pont or in the vicinity, as well as in most frequented places, and they display beautiful vessels containing the rarest medicaments."[64]

In one of the boats on the river a fisherman lifts a fish from a crate to show a prospective customer. Innumerable fast days in the mediaeval calendar created a demand for "all sorts of succulent fresh fish which on fast days satisfy people's temperate appetites just as on other days rich meats combined with rare, piquant sauces gratify their fastidious tastes."[65]

Plate IX. II, fol. 129 ro. (detail)

A blind beggar is led past the shops of the money changer and the goldsmith on the Grand Pont by a dog carrying an alms bowl in its mouth. Approaching the Cité along the Petit Pont, a workman with a hod slung over his shoulder follows a man who raises a warning finger toward the guard in a tower.

Below on the Seine a shipment of lumber is being unloaded from two ships. Here again the artist has placed the scene at the Grand Pont instead of at La Grève.

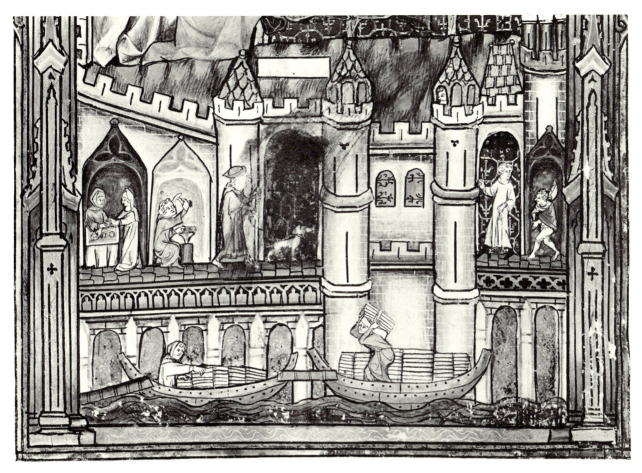

Plate X. ii, fol. 130 vo. (detail)

Two boatloads of charcoal are being readied for their arrival in Paris, where they would be met by porters. These "carefree roustabouts carrying sacks of charcoal in La Grève have hearts so light that difficulties don't bother them. They work in patience, dancing, skipping, jumping, and go to Saint Marcel for tripe. Since they consider treasure not worth three pipes, they spend all their wages and savings in the tavern, then go back to carry their burdens, but with joy, not misery. They earn their bread lawfully, without stooping to robbery and theft, and then go back to the cask and drink, living as they ought."[66]

The transportation of another import is depicted on the Grand Pont where a cart, laden with a cask of wine, is pulled toward the gate to the Cité by four men in harness while another man supervises.

South of the Cité on the Petit Pont, a barefoot pilgrim, his shoes slung over his shoulder, carrying a staff and begging bowl, is briskly setting out or returning from a pilgrimage. Men had long been taught to be charitable to pilgrims. The twelfth century "baedeker" for pilgrims to Saint-Jacques-de-Compostelle told tales of what happened to those who neglected this duty: "Pilgrims, poor or rich, returning from Saint-Jacques or on their way there, ought to be received with charity and consideration by everyone; because whoever eagerly receives them and gives them lodging will have as their guest not only Saint Jacques but our Saviour; for the gospel has said, 'Whosoever receives you receives me.' Many have incurred the wrath of God because they did not wish to receive a pilgrim of Saint-Jacques and the poor. . . . At Villeneuve, a poor pilgrim of Saint-Jacques spoke to a woman who was tending bread in hot coals. He begged food for the love of God and the blessed Jacques, but she replied that she had no bread. At that the pilgrim exclaimed, 'May it please heaven to change your bread into stone.' When the pilgrim had departed and gone a good distance the mean woman went to take her bread from the coals and found in its place a round stone. Struck with contrition she immediately went in search of the pilgrim, but could not find him. . . . This is why everyone ought to know that rich or poor, pilgrims of Saint-Jacques deserve hospitality and a sincere welcome."[67]

44

Plate XI. III, fol. 1 ro. (detail)

In the mediaeval Paris of only two bridges, boats were used constantly for getting from one part of the city to another. Here, as in several other miniatures, two men are boating on the river; in every case the boatmen use only one paddle.

A man drives a wagon filled with stones across the Grand Pont. This type of two wheeled wagon with shafts came into being with the invention of the modern horse traction-harness. The new way of harnessing made it possible for one horse, instead of two, to draw a wagon. If one was not strong enough for the load, another was harnessed to the shafts to pull in tandem as in this scene.

Two cripples, crawling and hobbling on crutches, enter the Cité from the Petit Pont.

Plate XII. III, fol. 2 vo. (detail)

A fisherman makes a catch from a boat on the Seine. Above on the bridges, a supervisor directs a group of men pulling with ropes a wine cask onto runners, and a water carrier with two buckets suspended from a pole over his shoulders proceeds on his rounds. Delivery of water was an important occupation in mediaeval Paris; thirty-seven of these carriers are listed in the tax register of 1297.[68]

Plate XIII. III, fol. 4 vo. (detail)

On his way into Paris a postilion cracks a whip over the lead horse pulling a wagon, loaded with sheaves of wheat, through the gate at the end of the Grand Pont. A man carrying a sheep over his shoulder crosses the Petit Pont, probably on his way to the slaughterhouse located on the Right Bank, outside the main part of the city, because of the unpleasant smells and pollution it created.[69]

Alongside the Grand Pont two boatloads of pumpkins have arrived from the country.[70]

Plate XIV. III, fol. 6 vo. (detail)

Spring seems to have come to Paris. Passing the shops of the money changer and the goldsmith, a street musician strolls along the Grand Pont. He plays a portable organ, the popular instrument "that could be carried in one hand while he himself worked the bellows and played. . . ."[71] A youth lazily stretches out in a boat moored to the Petit Pont where a man is napping in a doorway.

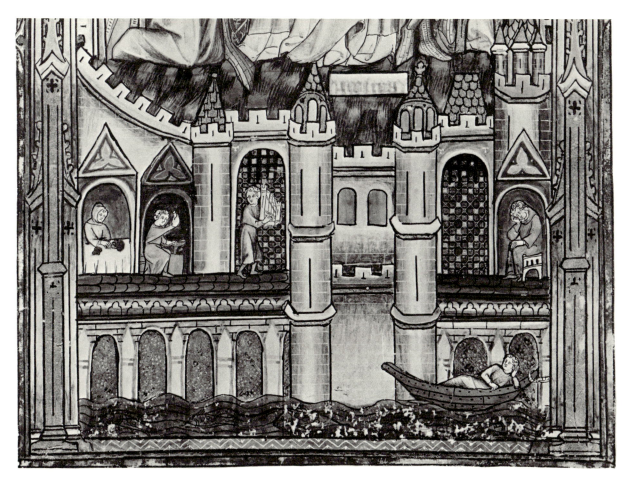

Plate XV. III, fol. 8 vo. (detail)

A cripple with an amputated leg hobbles on crutches along the Grand Pont toward a woman transacting business with a money changer.

Most well-to-do mediaeval households included grooms for dogs whose duty was to feed, exercise, and even sleep with their charges.[72] One of these grooms is shown here taking a pair of hounds for an outing on the Petit Pont.

In warm weather swimming was a favorite Parisian sport. Two men are undressing in a boat while a naked youth, holding his nose, prepares to jump into the river where two companions are already swimming. The naked youth clearly has a tail! Did the French artist intend to represent an Englishman in satiric allusion to the student gibe that "the English are drunkards and have tails"?[73]

Plate XVI. III, fol. 10 vo. (detail)

A boat passes the Grand Pont where the money changer and the goldsmith are at work. The Petit Pont is
deserted except for a man enjoying a siesta.

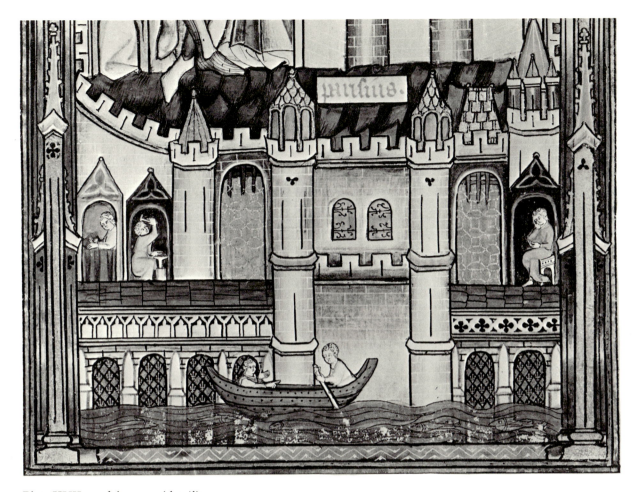

Plate XVII. III, fol. 12 vo. (detail)

A lazy atmosphere pervades this river scene; a man dreamily leaning on a wine cask seems content to let his boat drift along. Above on the Grand Pont two muleteers drive their beasts of burden toward the gate leading into the Cité. On the Petit Pont a woman winds wool in her house or shop.

Plate XVIII. III, fol. 14 vo. (detail)

A boatman paddles along the river below the bridges where three men are gathered around a cart loaded with a keg of wine, and a groom leads a smartly stepping horse toward the Cité.

Plate XIX. III, fol. 16 vo. (detail)

On Saturdays, when the market was held in Paris, the bridges were crowded with peasants from the country bringing their produce and animals into the city. Some things were subject to toll on the Petit Pont, others at the market itself or at the weighing station.[74] Here a shepherd guiding a flock of sheep and a swineherd driving a pig enter the gates of the Cité, while on the river below a shipment of melons arrives.

Plate XX. III, fol. 18 vo. (detail)

A load of wine casks is brought into the Cité on a cart pulled across the Grand Pont by two horses in tandem. From a boat on the river a man is peacefully fishing, undisturbed by the street fight in progress on the Petit Pont. Jean de Jandun found Parisians "endowed with such moderation and gentleness that, through admirable habit, they rarely become angry; but those that depart from the middle road transgress rather by violence than by apathy[!]."[75]

Plate XXI. III, fol. 20 vo. (detail)

Two men are boating on the Seine below the Grand Pont, where a herdsman goads his oxen toward the bridge gate. On the Petit Pont a porter delivers a sack to a man standing outside his shop or house. A Parisian householder warned his young wife against these porters: "Some there be that be hired as workmen for a fixed time to perform some short piece of work, as porters who carry burdens on their backs, wheelbarrow men, packers and the like; . . . they be necessary for the unloading and carrying of burdens and the doing of heavy work; and these be commonly tiresome, rough and prone to answer back, arrogant, haughty (save on pay day), and ready to break into insults if you do not pay them what they ask when the work is done . . . always bargain with them before they set hand to the work. . . ."[76]

Plate XXII. III, fol. 22 vo. (detail)

A blind man wearing a bell around his neck and leaning on a staff is led along the Grand Pont by a companion. These handicapped people were a source of amusement in the Middle Ages[77] and, the money changer watching from behind his counter may, like Guillaume de Villeneuve, have laughed at "the blind who cry at the top of their voices for bread for the inmates of the Champ Pourri"[78] where St. Louis had established a hospice for the blind. In the gate of the Petit Pont a woman is spinning while a pet monkey crouches nearby.

Two cargoes of wine arrive in Paris. From the stern of one of the boats a man directs his companion in the prow of the other boat.

Plate XXIII. III, fol. 24 vo. (detail)

Another shipment of wine is being towed into the city beneath the Grand Pont crossed by four porters carrying bundles of wood on their shoulders. In a shop at the end of the Petit Pont an apothecary, using two pestles, grinds his drugs. Not everyone shared Jean de Jandun's admiration for this profession. The author of the *Contrefait de Renard* complained that the apothecary says to his clients: " 'This comes from beyond the sea; it was sent at great cost because there is none of it in this country. This came from Armenia and this from Rome, that is from Acre and that from Nimes, this was brought from Damascus and this came from Saint Quentin.' And all of it grows in his own garden!"[79]

Plate XXIV. III, fol. 28 ro. (detail)

Passing the shops of the money changer and the gold-smith on the Grand Pont, a man carrying a golden cup and a jug cries the wine of one of the city's taverns. The streets of Paris were noisy with the calls of peddlers, and the noisiest were the wine criers.[80] In addition to those employed by taverns, others auctioned off newly imported wine:

> "Le bon vin fort a trente-deux
> A seize, a douze, a six, a huit."[81]

When an especially fine cargo arrived from distant parts the event was announced by a procession of criers.[82]

A peddler with two baskets of bread walks along the Petit Pont, beneath which a man sleeps in a boat moored to one of its piers.

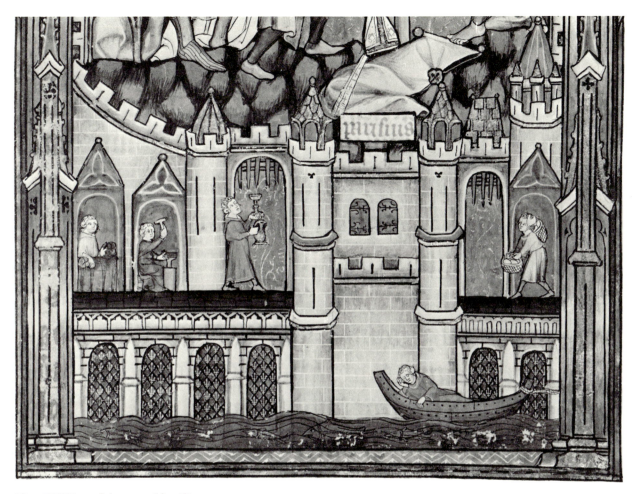

Plate XXV. III, fol. 30 ro. (detail)

Entering the gate at the end of the Grand Pont, a man straining in the shafts pulls a cart piled with sacks while another man pushes it from behind.

"From morning to night," we are told "the peddler of old boots and old shoes goes on his rounds" in the streets of Paris.[83] One of these peddlers, carrying a pair of shoes in one hand and a sack over his shoulder, crosses the Petit Pont; below on the river two young men converse in a boat.

Plate XXVI. III, fol. 32 ro. (detail)

A crowd has gathered on the Grand Pont to watch a performing bear. The animal stands on its forepaws at the command of a trainer, as a woman member of the troupe solicits money from one of the bystanders. Although traveling entertainers had been banned by Philippe Auguste, they came flocking back after his death and continued to delight their audiences, which for a few coins could "see monkeys, bears, dogs and marmosets put through their paces."[84] The thirteenth-century writer Jean Renart describes one of these troupes. "There are twenty people, then a hundred who make the lions and the bears roar. In the town's central square one plays the viol, another sings, one tumbles, and another entertains."[85]

Immune to the festive spirit of a group of men drinking wine in a boat moored to the Petit Pont, a porter trudges across the bridge carrying on his shoulder a basket filled with loaves of bread, that celebrated Parisian product. Already in the fourteenth century Parisian bakers were famous "above all others for an amazing superiority in their art resulting from the materials they use, the wheat and water so much better than other kinds; for this reason their bread acquires an incredible degree of goodness and delicacy. And most valuable of all the combination of these two qualities."[86]

Plate XXVII. III, fol. 33 vo. (detail)

On the Grand Pont the money changer awaits business, while next door the indefatigable goldsmith hammers on, and a ragpicker carrying a basket and pick passes beneath the raised portcullis into the Cité.

From a boat on the river a fisherman, escaping the cares of city life, casts his line toward a swarm of fish.

Outside an apothecary shop on the Petit Pont a doctor gives instruction for a prescription, possibly for "the herb scelerata macerated and kneaded with pig dung."[87] This cure for scrofulous tumors and boils was apparently one of the "effective, tested and appropriate remedies" which won Jean de Jandun's admiration for doctors, and with which "Aided by God and spring weather they rejoice in being able to restore in men their natural delight in living."[88]

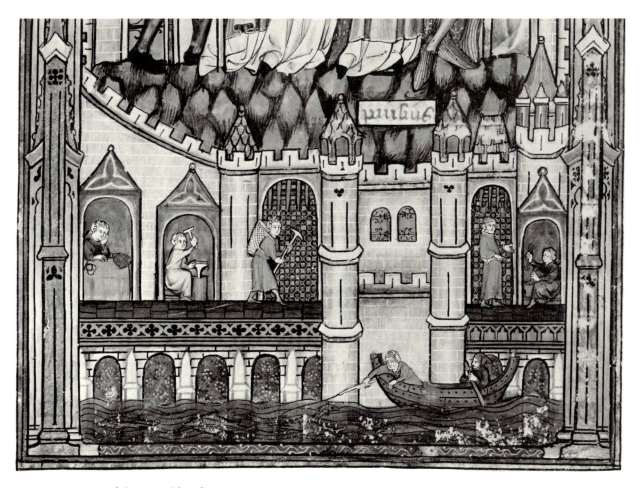

Plate XXVIII. III, fol. 35 vo. (detail)

For centuries the mills under the Grand Pont[89] and later those of the Pont-aux-Meuniers produced most of the flour for the city of Paris. This miniature depicts the delivery of grain to the mills. From a boat a man lifts a sack of grain to a miller seated in a small hut above one of the water wheels supported on boats beneath the bridge. Another man with a sack over his shoulder climbs a ladder to the mill under the third arch. This stone bridge, with its mills, is probably intended to represent the Grand Pont, before its destruction in 1296, and not the Pont-aux-Meuniers. The latter, as we noted earlier, was built of wood on the ruins of the Grand Pont and must have looked more as it is portrayed in a fifteenth-century book of Hours (fig. 36).

36. The Pont-aux-Meuniers. Hours, Manchester, John Rylands Library, MS lat. 164, fol. 254 ro.

Plate XXIX. III, fol. 37 vo. (detail)

"Warm patties, really hot! Warm pastries, scorching hot!"[90] was a cry frequently heard in the streets of Paris as peddlers called their "patties of pork, chicken and eel, seasoned with pepper; tarts and custard pies filled with soft cheese and eggs, fresh and sometimes not so fresh."[91] The money changer and a guard peering from a window of the bridge gate watch two of these peddlers setting off across the Grand Pont with their pastries on boards balanced over their shoulders. In a shop on the Petit Pont a barber shaves a customer. Many barbers, including some women, were listed in the tax registers of 1292[92] and 1313.[93]

Below the bridges a boat loaded with kegs of wine passes along the river.

Plate XXX. III, fol. 42 ro. (detail)

The series of scenes in Paris comes to an end with the departure of St. Denis to his place of martyrdom on Montmartre outside the city gates. Although this manuscript was intended for the king, the illuminators made no attempt to present a flattering picture of Paris as did a contemporary who wrote, "In name Paris differs little from Paradise because in reality she differs little."[94] Instead, these miniatures give an everyday and, with the exception of the architecture of the bridges, a generally accurate view of early fourteenth-century Paris. This is no "earthly Paradise"[95] but a city where practical interests of commerce and the importation of food, wine and fuel were of primary importance. Both the seamy and the lighthearted aspects of the city's life are emphasized—by beggars, cripples, and blind men on the one hand, and by people enjoying sports and amusements on the other.[96] The king would have recognized here the Paris he observed from his palace windows or as he rode across the bridges.

In this manuscript religious and secular miniatures, Latin and vernacular texts, are combined in a new way. Genre figures, it is true, had often been associated with religious subjects but they had usually been relegated to incidental sculptures on churches or to marginal illustrations in manuscripts. Here, however, the genre figures are given a prominent place in the miniatures portraying the life of St. Denis; these figures, no longer isolated, are placed in scenes with architectural settings intended to represent actual sites in Paris. This marks a radical innovation, a kind of illustration that would not become common for another hundred years.[97]

Notes

1 The inscriptions on the scrolls held by Abbot Gilles and the king read: "We offer you this written record of your good patron's deeds"; "We are grateful to you for this account of the ordeals of so great a father." Philippe does not hold a scepter, only the hand of justice, that royal symbol first used by his recently deceased brother Louis X.

2 MS fr. 2090-2092, I, fol. 3 ro. ". . . ut iam pie recordationis progeniter vester mortuus sit et quasi non mortuus dum in vobis non solum nomine sed dignitate et devotione filium sibi similem dereliquit."

3 L. Delisle, "Notice sur un recueil historique présenté à Philippe le long par Gilles de Pontoise, abbé de Saint-Denis," *Notices et extraits des manuscrits de la bibliothèque impériale*, XXI, pt. 2, 1865, 249ff.

4 On fol. A vo., one reads, ". . . libellum presentem, . . . per dilectum fratrem ac venerabilem commonachum nostrum Yvonem, cui et hoc ipsum commisimus, tanquam perhumilem et devotum obedience filium, studiose ac veraciter elaboratum . . . vestre regie majestati humiliter afferre decrevi." Félibien also mentions Abbot Gilles's commission to Yves; see M. Félibien, *Histoire de l'abbaye royale de Saint-Denis en France*, Paris, 1706, 269.

5 Bibliothèque Nationale, MS lat. 13836, fol. 124 vo.

6 Bibliothèque Nationale, MS fr. 2700, fol. 8 vo. "La vie saint Denys et la vie de XLVI autres sains, bien ystoriée, a chemise de toille."

7 Bibliothèque Nationale, MS fr. 2700, fol. 59 ro. "Item, la vie saint Denis et la vie quarante-six autre sains, bien historiez, à chemise de toile à queue, escript de lettre formée, en françois et latin, commencant on II fo. *nobis ut mundi*, et on derrenier *donnant aux royaulx*; a II fermouers d'argent dorez." Elizabeth Beatson has pointed out to me that a "chemise à queue" was a loose outer cover, for protecting the binding, with a "tail" which could be slipped through one's belt or grasped in one's hand for convenience in carrying the book.

8 L. Delisle, *Recherches sur la librairie de Charles V*, Paris, 1907, I, 30f., 137.

9 I am grateful to M. Meurgey de Tupigny for his identification of the lion passant of Laval which had puzzled Delisle and which the latter identified as that of Guyenne (Delisle, "Notice sur un recueil historique," 253, note 2).

10 A. Lecoy de la Marche, *Le Roi René, sa vie, son administration, ses travaux artistiques et littéraires*, Paris, 1875, II, 183.

11 Quatrebarbes, *Oeuvres complètes du roi René*, Angers, I, 1845, 109.

12 L. Delisle, *Le Cabinet des manuscrits de la bibliothèque impériale*, Paris, I, 1868, 268f. Hippolyte's father, Philippe de Bethune, also a collector of books, served briefly, circa 1602, in the government of Brittany. If the *Life of St. Denis* was still preserved in Laval, could he have acquired it at this time?

13 It contains chapters 57 to 168 of the third part.

14 This may be the "Chronique de France, fol. bois, écrit sur parchemin avec images" listed in M. Thévenot, *Catalogue des manuscrits de la bibliothèque de defunt Monseigneur le chancelier Seguier*, Paris, 1686, Inv. des mss., 16.

15 Vol. I: 5¾ x 9¼ inches; vol. II: 5¾ x 9¼ inches; vol. III: 5¾ x 9½ inches. For a few instances of cutting see vol. I, fol. 5 ro. where the inscription in the margin has been cut, and on fols. 1 ro. and 23 ro. the tops of the pen flourishes have been cut.

16 Fol. 135 vo.
"O genus insigne rex qui preclara benigne
regna philippe regis francor tramite legis
regalis voti guillermi pennula scoti
librum scripsit ita de patroni tibi vita
et regerum gestis; quibus est hystoria testis
et de regali successu. nobile quali regnat honore dei
nunc usq: genus clodovei et karoli magni
vestigia penitus agni in te preclare sequit

rex percipe gnare hanc per scripturam cui debes
tradere curam
per .C.ter.d.bis.septem tempus habebis."
One wonders whether this Guillaume l'Escot is the
one mentioned in the tax register of 1297 as living
near the house of Jehan l'Escrivain; see K. Michaëlsson, "Le Livre de la taille de Paris l'an 1297," *Göte-*
borgs universitets årsskrift, LXVII, 1961, no. 3, 361.

17 Delisle considered the two manuscripts as creations
of the same workshop, but not parts of the same
manuscript. He believed that MS fr. 2090-2092 was
the volume presented to Philip in 1317, and that MS
lat. 13836 was another copy (Delisle, "Notice sur
un recueil historique," 253, 257, 260). Although Vitzthum in 1907 (G. Vitzthum, *Die Pariser Miniatur-*
malerei, Leipzig, 1907, 170, 185ff.) described MS lat.
13836 as the last volume of MS fr. 2090-2092, Martin
in his monograph, a year later, wrote that the third
part of the *Life of St. Denis* had been lost (H. Martin,
Légende de Saint Denis, Paris, 1908, 4, 11). This latter belief was repeated in a catalogue of the Bibliothèque Nationale (*Les Manuscrits à peintures en*
France du XIIIe au XVIe siècle, Paris, 1955, 23). Morand has called MS lat. 13836 "a sister MS" of MS fr.
2090-2092 (K. Morand, *Jean Pucelle,* Oxford, 1962,
45). Nordenfalk shares Vitzthum's opinion but believes MS lat. 13836 reveals a different hand (C. Nordenfalk, "Maitre Honoré et Maitre Pucelle," *Apollo,*
LXXIX, 1964, 363). Avril has stated that MS lat. 13836
may possibly be a fragment of MS fr. 2090-2092 (Bibliothèque Nationale, *La Librairie de Charles V,* Paris,
1968, 79f. [149]). Marie Montpetit states that it might
be the third part of MS fr. 2090-2092, although written
by a different scribe and illustrated by another artist
(The National Gallery of Canada, *Art and the Courts,*
France and England, 1259-1328, Ottawa, 1972, 82).

18 MS fr. 2090-2092, III, fol. 111 vo.

19 The illustrations were left unfinished; later in the second half of the fifteenth century more drawings were
added. Nordenfalk has made the interesting suggestion
that this manuscript may have been the work of one
of Pucelle's assistants and that, while MS fr. 2090-2092
was being copied in the shop, Pucelle himself, with
characteristic use of perspective and chiaroscuro, may

have painted over the sarcophagus in the miniature in
III, fol. 53 vo. A photograph taken by transmitted
light shows the original underpainting of a sarcophagus treated in a flat manner, with neither perspective
nor chiaroscuro, similar in style to the rest of the
manuscript. Since Nordenfalk made this suggestion,
F. Baron has found evidence that Pucelle was dead by
1334. If Pucelle and an assistant were indeed respon-
sible for this overpainting and for MS lat. 5286, this
manuscript would be dated between 1317 and 1334.

20 The mediaeval Louvre probably looked very much as
it is depicted in the *Très Riches Heures.* In a lecture,
Professor Meiss compared the miniature of the château
of Saumur in that manuscript with a photograph of
the building still in existence; he commented that, except for a tendency toward attenuation, the Lim-
bourgs' architectural drawings were probably quite
accurate.

21 These thirteenth-century piers were strengthened and
redecorated in the early fourteenth century before
Jean Ravy began to build the present flying buttresses
around the choir and apse. The restoration here by
Viollet le Duc probably followed quite closely the
original work. See M. Aubert, *Notre-Dame de Paris,*
Paris, 1920, 174ff.; *Eugène Viollet le Duc 1814-1879,*
Paris, 1965, no. 141, pl. 29.

22 Records of the University of Paris include the name
of Thomas de Wymonduswold among the copyists
who conformed to their rules; see P. Durrieu, "Un
Siècle de l'histoire de la miniature parisienne à partir
du règne de Saint Louis," *Journal des savants,* n.s.
VII, 1909, 17.

23 Compare two men fighting, the ragpicker, and the
beggar carrying a baby on his back in MS lat. 3893,
fols. 97 ro., 197 vo., and 207 vo. with MS fr. 2090-
2092, III, fols. 20 vo., 35 vo., and II, fol. 11 ro. K.
Morand, in her unpublished Ph.D. dissertation, *Jean*
Pucelle and His Workshop, London, University of
London, 1958, 77 sees in fols. 218 ro. to 229 vo. of
MS lat. 3893 a style which she considers a direct fore-
runner of that in the *Life of St. Denis.*

24 I am grateful to François Avril for telling me about
this interesting manuscript, which he will probably
publish.

25 I am again indebted to François Avril for bringing these manuscripts to my attention. The Decretals of Gratian, MS 3898 in the Bibliothèque Nationale, was attributed by Vitzthum to the same workshop which produced MS fr. 2090-2092 (Vitzthum, *Pariser Miniaturmalerei*, 190ff.). Although the faces are somewhat similar, the proportions of the figures and some of the elaborate background ornament are quite different.

26 L. Delisle, "Les Heures de Blanche de France, duchesse d'Orléans," *Bibliothèque de l'école des chartes*, LXVI, 1905, 489-539. Avril and Morand, however, believe that Spencer 56 should be dated earlier in the century. At least two hands are apparent in the early fourteenth-century miniatures; the calendar of the first six pages was added at the beginning of the fifteenth century, and folios VII-XXX, 390-423 belong to a later date, probably the end of the fourteenth century.

27 She was a great-grandniece of St. Louis. The special emphasis on this saint in the Hours would therefore be particularly appropriate. Although Morand, in her Ph.D. dissertation, *Jean Pucelle*, 97f., note 1, said that since she had not seen Spencer 56 she preferred to leave the question of its original ownership open, she did suggest that it might have belonged to Philippe V's daughter Blanche who entered the Franciscan convent of Longchamp in 1315 and died in 1358, or to St. Louis' daughter Blanche who died in 1320. The one would have prayed for her father Philippe V, the other for her nephew Philippe le Bel or her great nephew Philippe V. It seems unlikely, however, that the prayers were for "King" Philippe because besides the prayers for Philippe there are others for the king (without naming him).

28 The young boy died in 1321; on March 24 of that year the king ordered a gift of grain to be given annually to the nurse of the deceased Philippe, who was buried at the abbey of Pont-aux-Dames-de-Crecy; see P. Anselme, *L'Histoire genéalogique de la maison de France*, Paris, I, 1726, 96.

29 J.-M. Richard, *Une Petite-Nièce de Saint Louis Mahaut comtesse d'Artois et de Bourgogne*, Paris, 1887, 99, note 1.

30 K. Michaëlsson, "Le Livre de la taille de Paris, l'an de grace 1313," *Göteborgs hogskolas årsskrift*, LVII, 1951, no. 3, 119.

31 B. Prost, "Liste des artistes mentionnés dans les états de la maison du roi et des maisons des princes, du XIIIe siècle à l'an 1500," *Archives historiques, artistiques et littéraires*, I, 1889-1890, 426.

32 Nordenfalk, "Maître Honoré," 364. Nordenfalk attributes MSS fr. 2090-2092 and lat. 248 to Maciot's workshop. He believes that Maciot can be identified with Jaquet Maci who collaborated with Pucelle on the Billyng Bible, but Martin thought not since Maci was such a common name (Martin, *Légende*, 29).

33 The iconography of the Billyng Bible, signed by Pucelle, Jaquet Maci, and Anciau de Cens, closely follows MS lat. 248, and the caryatids in the latter's Genesis page may have suggested those in the Hours at the Cloisters of the Metropolitan Museum usually identified as the Hours executed for Jeanne d'Evreux by Pucelle between 1325 and 1328 (see K. Morand, *Jean Pucelle*, Oxford, 1962, 42, 45). Although doubts have been cast on the attribution of the Cloisters' Hours to Pucelle (see R. Blum, "Jean Pucelle et la miniature parisienne du XIVe siècle," *Scriptorium*, III, 1949, 211-217; F. Deuchler, "Jean Pucelle, Facts and Fictions," *Metropolitan Museum of Art Bulletin*, XXIX, 1971, 253-256; and E. Flinn, "A Magnificent Manuscript—a Historical Mystery," *ibid.*, 255-260), I do not think that the case against Pucelle has been proved.

Compare:

	Hours of Jeanne d'Evreux	MS fr. 2090-2092
Crucified Christ	fol. 68 vo.	I, fol. 34 ro.
Water carrier	fol. 19 vo.	III, fol. 4 vo.
Leper begging	fol. 20 ro.	II, fol. 129 ro.
Doctor and patient	fol. 143 ro.	II, fol. 125 ro.

Compare the triple pinnacled piers of the architectural frames enclosing the miniatures of MS fr. 2090-2092 with those in the frontispiece of the Bible Historiale, MS fr. 2, fol. 1 ro. in the Bibliothèque Publique et Universitaire of Geneva, attributed to Pucelle, circa 1330.

Morand, in her Ph.D. dissertation, *Jean Pucelle*,

55ff. traces the influence of MSS lat. 248, fr. 2090-2092, and lat. 13836 on the Breviary of Blanche of France (Vatican Library, MS Urb. lat. 603), the Hours of Jeanne de Savoy (Paris, Musée Jacquemart-André), and the Billyng Bible (Paris, Bibliothèque Nationale, MS lat. 11935).

34 "Surtout garde les bonnes villes . . . car, par la force et par les richesses des grosses villes, douteront li privé et li estrange de mespenre vers toy, especialment ti per ti baron" (J. de Joinville, *Histoire de Saint Louis*, ed. N. de Wailly, Paris, 1874, 404 [749]).

35 "Anno Domini M CC nonagesimo sexto, pluvia continua, absque gelu et nive, Parisius tantum inundaverunt aque quod Pontem Minorem cum domibus et partem magnem Castelleti juncti ponti ipsi, festo beati Thome apostoli subverterunt et etiam totum Magnum Pontem cum omnibus domibus usque ad domum proximam ecclesis Sancti Lefredi horribiliter secum vexerunt et fundamenta desuper in ostensione posuerunt. . . . Facti sunt pontes lignei; primo populus transivit par Parvum Pontem. iiii kal. maii hoc est die beati Vitalis martyris hoc fuit prima dominica post octavam Pasche, vigilia Robert abbatis. . . . Populus transivit primo per Magnem Pontem crastino beati Martini hyemalis hoc est vigilia Brictii" (A. Vernet, "L'Inondation de 1296-1297 à Paris," *Mémoires de la fédération des sociétés historiques et archéologiques de Paris et de l'Ile de France*, I, 1949, 49f.).

36 The old bridge connected the palace on the Cité with the Grande Rue or the Rue St. Denis on the Right Bank.

37 A. Berty, "Recherches sur l'origine et la situation du Grant Pont de Paris, du Pont aux Changeurs, du Pont aux Meuniers et de celui de Charles le Chauve," *Revue archéologique*, XII, 1855, pt. I, 197, 210. Berty quotes from a 1323 entry in the archives of the Chapter of Notre-Dame, "que l'entrée du pont que l'en appelloit le pont des Moulins, estoit assis par devers Saint-Leffroy."

38 This was the arrangement of the early bridges described by Abbon, *Le Siège de Paris par les normands, poème du IXe siècle*, ed. and trans. by H. Waquet, Paris, 1942, 14: "Dextra tui pontes habitant tentoria limfe Levaque claudentes; horum hinc inde tutrices Cis urbem speculare falas citra quoque flumen."

39 An ordonnance of February 1304 assigned the Exchange ". . . super nostrum magnum Pontum solummodò, a parte Gravie, inter ecclesiam Sancti Leofredi et *majorem arcam*" (italics mine) and stipulated "nulli omnino liceat alibi quam in loco illo Cambiare." See *Ordonnances des roys de France . . .*, Paris, I, 1723, 426.

40 *Ibid.*

41 *Ibid.*, I, 1723, 714f.

42 Michaëlsson, "Le Livre de la taille, 1313," 150.

43 The building of the Petit Pont was described in the twelfth century by Godfroi sub-prior of the abbey of Saint-Victor in Paris: "Des hommes ont construit un pont de leurs propres mains et ont créé un passage commode au-dessus du fleuve; ils ont établi des maisons pour chacun d'eux; et c'est de la qu'ils ont pris le nom d'habitants du pont (Parvi-Pontins). Les matériaux n'en sont moins beaux que l'architecture; le dessous du pont est formé de piles en pierres taillées, et cette solide structure est appuyée sur des colonnes fortes comme l'airain, qui défient à jamais tous les chocs. Le dessus du pont est garni de pavés biens unis, décoré d'enseignes d'or et d'argent (dorées et argentées), muni des deux côtés de murs assez élevés pour que la foule inexpérimentée n'ait pas de chute à redouter. Mais il y a aussi des saillies ou ouvrages extérieurs (exedras), au moyen desquels on peut voir l'eau du fleuve et en sonder la profondeur cachée. Quelques-uns viennent se livrer aussi en cet endroit au plaisir de la natation et refraichir leurs membres brûlées par les ardeurs de l'été. Là se tient une école de docteurs vénérables, éminents par leur science et leurs moeurs, qui instruisent les populations ignorantes. Heureux le peuple qui a de tels maîtres" (Le Roux de Lincy and L. Tisserand, *Paris et ses historiens*, Paris, 1867, 14f.; original Latin text in note 1, p. 15).

44 "Aussi avint de ceste chose comme qui averoit demain boutei le feu (dont Diex le gart!) à Petit-Pont de Paris" (de Joinville, *Histoire*, 90 [164]).

45 ". . . ex variis mundi partibus opulentias humanis usibus oportunas uberrime submisistrat. Vina etenim

Grecie, Varnacie, Rupelle, Vasconie, Borgundie, copiose deportat. Triticum siliginem, pisa, fabas, fenum, advenam, sal, carbones et ligna propinat ad plenum" (Le Roux de Lincy and Tisserand, *Paris*, 56).

46 C. Haskins, *Studies in Mediaeval Culture*, Oxford, 1929, 57; quotation from the collection of sermons delivered by Robert de Sorbonne in 1260-1261 (MS lat. 15971 in the Bibliothèque Nationale).

47 See note 43.

48 "Li singes au marchant doit IIII deniers, se il pour vendre le porte; et se li singes est à home qui l'ait acheté por son déduit, si est quites; et se li singes est au joueur, jouer en doit devant le paagier; et pour son jeu doit estre quites de toute chose qu'il achète à son usage; et ausi tot li jongleur sunt quite por. I. ver de chançon" (E. Boileau, *Réglemens sur les arts et métiers de Paris rédigés au XIIIe siècle et connus sous le nom du livre des métiers d'Etienne Boileau*, introduction and notes by G. Depping, Paris, 1837, 287). In a late thirteenth-century manuscript (MS fr. 24069, fol. 204 ro. in the Bibliothèque Nationale) of the *Livre des métiers* some crude drawings of a viol, the head of a jongleur, and two dancing monkeys were added in the early fourteenth century in the margin to illustrate this passage.

49 By representing the saint on the Grand Pont, the artist may have wished to give an aura of special importance to his arrival for this was the route to the Cité taken by French kings after their coronations at Saint Denis.

50 ". . . veniens ad palatii fenestras, unde fluvium Sequanae pro recreatione animi quandoque inspicere consueverat, rhedae equis trahentibus per civitatem transeuntes, foetores intolerabiles lutum revolvendo procreaverunt. Quod Rex in aula deambulans ferre non sustinens, arduum opus, sed valde necessarium, excogitavit, quod omnes praedecessores sui ex nimia gravitate et operis impensa aggredi non praesumpserant. Convocatis autem burgensibus cum praeposito ipsius civitatis, regia auctoritate praecepit quod omnes vici et viae totius civitatis Parisii duris et fertibus lapidibus sternerentur" (*Recueil des historiens des Gaules et de la France*, ed. M. J. J. Brial, Paris, XVII, 1878, 16).

51 Michaëlsson, "Le Livre de la taille, 1313," 69, 88.

52 Boileau, *Réglemens*, 262.

53 "Insuper metallicorum vasorum, precipue de auro et argento, stanno et cupro, figuratores optimi supra Pontem vocatum Magnum . . . malleos super incudes, quasi armonice concurrentibus ictibus, faciunt resonare" (Le Roux de Lincy and Tisserand, *Paris*, 54). The money changers and the goldsmiths were established on opposite sides of the Grand Pont (see above p. 22), which was lined on both sides by shops and houses. But throughout the manuscript, in order to show activity on the bridge, the artist has given a doll's house view.

54 "Mais en cest endroit d'espreveterie, le convient plus que devant tenir sur le poing et le porter aux plais et entre les gens aux églises et ès autres assemblées, et emmy les rues, et le tenir jour et nuit le plus continuelment que l'en pourra, et aucune fois le perchier emmy les rues pour veoir gens, chevaulx, charettes, chiens, et toutes choses congnoistre; . . ." (*Le Ménagier de Paris; traité de morale et d'économie domestique composé vers 1393 par un bourgeois Parisien*, Paris, 1846, II, 296).

55 "Tant poi i ai mis que j'avoie,
Tant que povretez me mestroie.
Après mise ma robe j'é.
Lecherie m'a desrobé;
Si ne sai mès que devenir,
Ne quel chemin puisse tenir.

. . . .

Par ces rues sont granz les presses,
Je vous di de ces genz menues,
Orrez crier parmi ces rues:
Menjue pain. Diex! qui m'apele?
Vien ça, vuide ceste escuele."
(G. A. Crapelet, *Proverbes et dictons populaires avec les dits du mercier et des marchands et les crieries de Paris aux XIIIe et XIVe siècles*, Paris, 1831, 145f., 141.)

56 Le Roux de Lincy and Tisserand, *Paris*, 42.

57 C. Dahlberg, *The Romance of the Rose*, Princeton, 1971, 106.

58 Jean de Jandun: "O quam graciosi sunt illi optimi medicorum . . ." (Le Roux de Lincy and Tisserand, *Paris*, 42).

59 Boileau, *Réglemens*, xxvi.

60 I have not been able to find out whether bird merchants were located on the Grand Pont in the early fourteenth century or whether the figure in this scene represents an itinerant peddler. A poem of 1325 speaks of merchants selling birds before the church of Ste.-Geneviève-la-Petite at the end of the Rue Neuve Notre-Dame. In April 1402 the bird merchants received permission to return to the Pont-au-Change (formerly called the Grand Pont) from the Vallée de Misère (between the Place du Châtelet and the Rue des Lavandières) because on the bridge they had more protection from the weather (A. Franklin, *La Vie privée d'autrefois*, Paris, XXIV, 1899, 225, 227f.). T. H. White made an amusing comment on bird merchants in a discussion of the caladrius, that bird which the Bestiaries tell us turned its back on a sick man about to die but faced the patient who would recover. A sick person had only to enter a bird shop, White wrote, to see if the caladrius looked at him or not and then he would leave without buying; few dealers, therefore, displayed their birds without cash down (T. H. White, *The Bestiary, A Book of Beasts*, New York, 1960, 116, note 1).

61 Gregory of Tours, *Historiae ecclesiasticae Francorum*, ed. and trans. by J. Guadet et Taranne, Paris, III, 1837, 218.

62 G. Raynaud and H. Lemaitre (eds.), *Le Roman de Renart le Contrefait*, Paris, 1914, 294 (156); P. Lehugeur, *Histoire de Philippe le Long*, Paris, 1897, 422ff.

63 L. MacKinney, "Double-pestle Action in Medieval Miniatures," *American Pharmaceutical Association Journal*, n.s. I, 1961, 161, 162. Compare similar representations in MS lat. 816, fol. 101 vo. in the Jagiellonska library, Cracow (late thirteenth-century *Varia in medicinam*) and MS gr. 2243, fol. 10 vo. in the Bibliothèque Nationale (Nicolas Myrepsos, *De compositione medicamentorum* of 1339).

64 Jean de Jandun wrote, "Apothecarii vero, qui de medicaminum materiis subserviunt, et aromaticarum specierum oblectamenta infinita conficiunt, super illum et juxta famosissimum vocatum Parvum Pontem, atque in ceteris plerisque locis patientibus, suorum vasorum, in quibus exquisita clauduntur medicamina, pulcritudines non occulant" (Le Roux de Lincy and Tisserand, *Paris*, 44).

65 Jean de Jandun wrote, ". . . tanta et tam recens, pinguis et bene sapida, utriusque maneriei, piscium copia propinatur, quod diebus, quibus ceterarum carnium usibus convenit abstinere, non minori commoditate reficitur sobrietas eorumdem, quam alibi alie sagininose pinguedines, curiosis salsarum pungentium acuminibus permixte, sufficere valeant faucibus delicatis" (Le Roux de Lincy and Tisserand, *Paris*, 76).

66 Dahlberg, *Romance*, 105f.

67 "Peregrini sive pauperes sive divites a liminibus Sancti Jacobi redientes, vel advientes, omnibus gentibus karitative sunt recipiendi et venerandi. Nam quicumque illos receperit et diligenter hospicio procuraverit, non solum beatum Jacobum, verum etiam ipsum Dominum hospitem habebit. Ipso Domino in evangelio dicente: 'Qui vos recipit me recipit.' Fuere olim multi qui iram Dei incurrerunt idcirco quia Sancti Jacobi peregrinos et egenos recipere noluerunt; . . . Apud Villamnovam, quidam Sancti Jacobi peregrinus egenus cuidam mulieri panem sub cineres calidos habenti, helemosinam amore Dei et beati Jacobi petivit; que respondit se panem non habere, cui peregrinus ait: 'Utinam panis quem habes, lapis esset!' Cumque peregrinus ille recedens a domo illa, longe distaret, acessit mulier illa nequam ad cineres, putans panem suum capere, lapidem rotundum in loco panis repperit. Que corde penitens ilico insecuta peregrinum non invenit. . . . Quapropter sciendum quod sancti Jacobi peregrini sive pauperes sive divites, jure sunt recipiendi et diligenter procurandi" (J. Viellard, *Le Guide du pèlerin de Saint-Jacques de Compostelle. Texte latin du XIIe siècle édité et traduit en français d'après les manuscrits de Compostelle et de Ripoll*, Macon, 1950, 122ff.).

68 K. Michaëlsson, "Le Livre de la taille de Paris l'an 1297," *Göteborgs universitets årsskrift*, LXVII, 1961, no. 3, 19, 184, 195, 219, 253, 256, 258, 265, 310, 317, 318, 323, 327, 333, 334, 335, 337, 345, 352, 367, 386, 397, 399, 401, 411.

69 Raoul de Presles writing in 1371 said that the slaughterhouses were outside the city "pour les punaises et

les corrupcions echiever" (Le Roux de Lincy and Tisserand, *Paris*, 95, 110).

70 Littré cites a thirteenth-century reference to pumpkins from Alebrant, "citroles sont froides plus que concombre."

71 Dahlberg, *Romance*, 343.

72 A. Franklin, *Dictionnaire historique des arts, métiers et professions*, Paris, 1906, 721; Richard, *Une Petite-Nièce*, 117f.

73 ". . . sed pro diversitate regionum mutuo dissidentes, invidentes et detrahentes, multas contra se contumelias et opprobria impudeter proferebant. Anglicos potatores et caudatos affirmantes" (Jacobi de Vitriaco, *Libri duo, quorum prior orientalis sive hierosolymitanae, alter occidentalis historiae inscribitur . . .* ed. D. Francisci Moschi, Duaci, 1597, 279).

74 Boileau, *Réglemens*, l.

75 ". . . tali utique mansuetudinis moderatione fruuntur, quod, ex laudabili consuetudine, mediocriter se habent ad irascendum: qui vero ipsorum declinat a medio, frequentius per iracundiam quam ire paucitatem transgrediuntur" (Le Roux de Lincy and Tisserand, *Paris*, 54).

76 E. Power (trans.), *The Goodman of Paris (le ménagier de Paris); A Treatise on Moral and Domestic Economy by a Citizen of Paris (c. 1393)*, London, 1928, 205f.

77 See *Le Garçon et l'aveugle*, a comedy played at Tournai between 1266 and 1288, cited by V.-L. Saulnier, *La Littérature française du moyen âge des origines à 1500*, Paris, 1948, 95.

78 "A pain crier metent grant paine;
Et li avvugle à haute alaine,
Du pain à cels de Champ porri,
Dont moult sovent, sachiez, me ri."
(Crapelet, *Proverbes*, 141.)

79 " 'Cecy vint de dela la mer;
A grant coust l'ay enveyé querre,
Car point n'en a en ceste terre.
Ceste est venue d'Hermenie,
Et ceste vint de Rommenie,
Celle d'Acre, celle de Nymes,
Ceste aporte de Damas fines

Et ceste de Saint Quentin!'
Et trestout crut en son jardin!"
(Raynaud and Lemaitre, *Renart*, II, 45.)

80 Crapelet, *Proverbes*, 137.

81 *Ibid.*, 142.

82 Boileau, *Réglemens*, lxiii.

83 Guillaume de Villeneuve:
". . . les viez housiaus,
Les sollers viez, et soir et main."
(Crapelet, *Proverbes*, 140.)

84 Quotation from *De la maille*:
"Si en voit l'en jouer les singes
Les ours, les chiens et les marmotes;

. . . .

Por la maaille seulement."
(A. Jubinal, *Jongleurs et trouvères*, Paris, 1835, 106.)

85 "La en a vint, la en a cent
Qui brere font lyons et ours;
En mi la ville, es quarrefours,
Viele cil et cist y chante,
Cil y tumbe, cist i enchante."
(J. Renart, *Galeran de Bretagne*, ed. L. Foulet, Paris, 1925, 103, vv. 3384-3388.)

86 Jean de Jandun: "De panis autem factoribus hoc interponere non pudet, quod vel ipsi mirabili artis prerogativa cunetis aliis sui generis dotati sunt, aut ipsorum materie, utpote grana et aqua, in tantum meliores sunt ceteris, ut, ob hoc, panes quos faciunt quasi incommensurabilem suscipiant bonitatis et delicationis excessum. Melius autem est si hoc ambe concurrant" (Le Roux de Lincy and Tisserand, *Paris*, 52, 54).

87 L. MacKinney, *Medical Illustrations in Medieval Manuscripts*, London, 1965, 37, cites this prescription from a thirteenth-century manuscript of the Pseudo-Apuleius' *Herbarium*.

88 ". . . per efficaces, expertas et proprias remediorum virtutes . . . in ipso vivere dulcedinem naturalem vitaleque Solatium resumendum, Deo et vere operantibus, gaudent se esse ministros" (Le Roux de Lincy and Tisserand, *Paris*, 42, 44).

89 These mills are referred to again and again in early records. The mill of Chanteraine (de Cantu rane), located at the end of the Grand Pont next to the Tour

de L'Horloge, is mentioned from 1248, that of the Bons-Hommes was sold in 1276 by the abbey of Saint-Cyr to the religious Bons-Hommes of the Bois de Vincennes. The monks of the Temple owned a mill under the Grand Pont from 1172. Between this mill and the one belonging from 1280 to the church of Sainte Opportune was the great arch through which boats passed; other mills were those of Saint Merry mentioned from 1280, one owned from 1070 by the priory of Saint-Martin-des-Champs, and another given in 1190 by Philippe Auguste to Saint Lazare. See Berty, "Recherches," 213.

90 "Chaus pastez i a, chaus gastiaux

. . .

Chaude oublées renforcies
Galetes chaudes, eschaudez."
(Crapelet, *Proverbes*, 139f.)

91 Jean de Garlande (beginning of the thirteenth century) speaks of the pastry makers "qui gagnent beaucoup en vendant des pâtés de porc, de volaille, d'anguille, assaisonnés de poivre, des tartes et des flans farcis de fromage mou, d'oeufs frais et parfois avancés." See P. Champion, *Splendeurs et misères de Paris, XIVe-XVe siècles*, Paris, 1934, 169.

92 P. Géraud, *Paris sous Philippe-le-Bel d'après des documents originaux*, Paris, 1837, 486.

93 Michaëlsson, "Le Livre de la taille, 1313," 6, 8, 13, 16, 22, 30, 36, 42, 50, 53, 54, 58, 66, 72, 76, 89, 92, 96, 123, 126, 127, 130, 137, 140, 144, 145, 162, 166, 170, 171, 187, 188, 201, 206, 211, 214, 218, 220, 226, 227, 230, 232, 234, 235, 236, 241, 242, 245, 248, 250, 258.

94 ". . . a Paradiso parum in nomine, et si non re . . ." (Le Roux de Lincy and Tisserand, *Paris*, 27).

95 Jean de Jandun: "terreni . . . Paradisi" (*ibid.*, 56).

96 Distribution of scenes in MS fr. 2090-2092: transportation, 29; amusements and leisure, 23; commerce, 22; craftsmen, 11; beggars and cripples, 7; bridge-gate watchmen, 6; medicine and barbering, 5; travel, 4; manual laborers, 2; millers, 1; pedestrian, 1.

97 About a hundred years later the interest in placing genre scenes in specific settings is well exemplified in the view of Venice in Marco Polo's *Li livres du Graunt Caam* (Oxford, Bodleian Library, MS Bodl. 264, fol. 218 ro.) and in the calendar miniatures of the *Très Riches Heures du Duc de Berry* (Chantilly, Musée Condé).

Bibliography

Abbon, *Le Siège de Paris par les Normands, poème du IXe siècle*, ed. and trans. by H. Waquet, Paris, 1942.

Anselme, P., *L'Histoire généalogique et chronologique de la maison royale de France*, Paris, 1726-1733. 9 vols.

Aubert, M., *Notre-Dame de Paris*, Paris, 1920.

d'Ayzac, F., *Histoire de l'abbaye de Saint-Denis*, Paris, 1860-1861. 2 vols.

Baer, L., "Pucelle," in Thieme-Becker, *Allgemeines Lexikon der Bildenden Künstler*, XXVII, 1933, 442, 443.

Baron, F., "Enlumineurs, peintres et sculpteurs parisiens des XIIIe et XIVe siècles d'après les roles de la taille," *Bulletin archéologique du comité des travaux historiques et scientifiques*, n.s. IV, 1968, 37-121.

——. "Enlumineurs, peintres et sculpteurs parisiens des XIVe et XVe siècles d'après les archives de l'hôpital Saint-Jacques-aux-Pèlerins," *Bulletin archéologique du comité des travaux historiques et scientifiques*, n.s., VI, 1970, 77-115.

Berty, A., "Recherches sur l'origine et la situation du Grand Pont de Paris, du Pont aux Changeurs, du Pont aux Meuniers et de celui de Charles le Chauve," *Revue archéologique*, XII, 1865, pt. I, 192-220.

——. *Topographie historique du vieux Paris*, Paris, 1866-1897. 6 vols.

Blum, R., "Jean Pucelle et la miniature parisienne du XIVe siècle," *Scriptorium*, III, 1949, 211-217.

Boileau, E., *Réglemens sur les arts et métiers de Paris rédigés au XIIIe siècle et connus sous le nom du livre des métiers d'Etienne Boileau*, avec notes et une introduction par G. B. Depping, Paris, 1837.

Boutaric, E., *La France sous Philippe le Bel*, Paris, 1861.

Buchon, J., *Collection des chroniques nationales françaises*, Paris, IX, 1827, *Chronique métrique de Godefroy de Paris suivie de la taille de Paris en 1313*.

Calliat, V., *Hôtel de ville de Paris* (mésuré, dessiné, gravé et publié par Victor Calliat. . . . Avec une histoire de ce monument et des recherches sur le gouvernement municipal de Paris par Le Roux de Lincy), Paris, 1844-1856. 2 vols. in one.

Champion, P., *Splendeurs et misères de Paris XIVe-XVe siècles*, Paris, 1934.

Cockerell, S., "The Parisian Miniaturist Honoré," *Burlington Magazine*, X, 1906-1907, 186, 191.

Couderc, C., *Album de portraits d'après les collections du département des manuscrits* (Bibliothèque Nationale), Paris, 1910.

——. *Les Enluminures des manuscrits du moyen âge (du VIe au XVe siècle) de la bibliothèque nationale*, Paris, 1927.

Crapelet, G. A., *Proverbes et dictons populaires avec les dits du mercier et des marchands et les crieries de Paris aux XIIIe et XIVe siècles*, Paris, 1831.

Dahlberg, C., trans., *The Romance of the Rose*, Princeton, 1971.

Delisle, L., "La Bible de Philippe le Bel," *Bibliothèque de l'école des chartes*, LV, 1894, 427-429.

——. *Le Cabinet des manuscrits de la bibliothèque impériale*, Paris, 1868-1881. 3 vols. and Plates.

——. "Les Heures de Blanche de France, duchesse d'Orléans," *Bibliothèque de l'école des chartes*, LXVI, 1905, 489-539.

——. "Notice sur un recueil historique presenté à Philippe le Long par Gilles de Pontoise, abbé de Saint-Denis," *Notices et extraits des manuscrits de la bibliothèque impériale*, XXI, pt. 2, 1865, 249-265.

——. *Recherches sur la librairie de Charles V*, Paris, 1907. 2 vols. and Portfolio.

Durrieu, P., "Les Armoiries du bon roi René," *Académie des inscriptions et belles-lettres, comptes rendu*, 1908, 102-104.

——. "Un Siècle de l'histoire de la miniature parisienne à partir du règne de Saint Louis," *Journal des savants*, n.s. VII, 1909, 5-19.

Ehrlich, B., *Paris on the Seine*, New York, 1962.

Evans, J., *Life in Medieval France*, London, 1957.

Fagniez, G., *Documents relatifs à l'histoire de l'industrie et du commerce en France*, Paris, 1898, 1900. 2 vols.

Faral, E., *Les Jongleurs en France au moyen âge*, Paris, 1910.

Félibien, M., *Histoire de l'abbaye royale de Saint-Denys en France . . .* , Paris, 1706.

Franklin, A., *Dictionnaire historique des arts, métiers et professions exercés dans Paris depuis le treizième siècle*, Paris, 1906.

————. *La Vie privée d'autrefois, arts et métiers, modes, moeurs, usages des Parisiens du XIIe au XVIIIe siècle*, Paris, 1887-1902. 27 vols.

Freyhan, R., "Ein Englischer Buchmaler in Paris zu Beginn des 14. Jahrhunderts," *Marburger Jahrbuch*, VI, 1931, 153-161.

Géraud, P., *Paris sous Philippe-le-Bel d'après des documents originaux*, Paris, 1837.

Gregory of Tours, *Historiae ecclesiasticae Francorum . . .* ed. and trans. by J. Guadet et Taranne, Paris, 1836-1838. 4 vols.

Guillaume de Nangis, *Chronique latine*, ed. by H. Géraud, Paris, 1843. 2 vols.

Haskins, C., *Studies in Mediaeval Culture*, Oxford, 1929.

————. "The University of Paris in the Sermons of the XIIIth Century," *The American Historical Review*, X, 1904, 1-27.

Hauréau, B., "Yves moine de Saint-Denis," *Histoire littéraire de la France*, XXI, 1893, 143-151.

Hinkle, W., "The Iconography of the Four Panels by the Master of Saint Gilles," *Journal of the Warburg and Courtauld Institutes*, XXVIII, 1965, 112-130.

Holmes, U. T., "The Monkey in Mediaeval Literature," *Studies in the Romance Languages and Literature*, University of North Carolina, no. 92, 1970, 93-100.

The Hours of Jeanne d'Evreux, Queen of France, at the Cloisters, Facsimile with introduction by James J. Rorimer, New York, 1957.

Jacobus de Vitriaco, *Libri duo, quorum prior orientalis sive hierosolymitanae, alter occidentalis historiae nomine inscribitur . . . omnia . . . studio et opera*, ed. D. F. Moschi, Douai, 1597.

Jal, A., *Glossaire nautique*, Paris, 1848. 2 vols.

Joinville, J. de, *Histoire de Saint Louis*, ed. N. de Wailly, Paris, 1874.

Jubinal, A., *Jongleurs et trouvères ou choix de saluts, épitres, rèveries et autres pièces légères des XIIIe et XIVe siècles*, Paris, 1835.

Lacroix, P., *France in the Middle Ages*, New York, 1963.

———— and F. Seré, *Le Moyen Age et la Renaissance, histoire et description des moeurs et usages, du commerce et de l'industrie*, Paris, 1848-1851.

Langlois, C., *La Vie en France au moyen âge*, Paris, 1924-1928. 4 vols.

Lavedan, P., *Les Villes françaises*, Paris, 1960.

Lebeuf, J., *Histoire de la ville et de tout le diocèse de Paris*, Paris, 1754. 15 vols. in 12; 1st vol. on Paris.

Le Clerc, J. and E. Renan, *Histoire littéraire de la France au quatorzième siècle*, Paris, 1865. 2 vols.

Lecoy de la Marche, A., *Le Roi René, sa vie, son administration, ses travaux artistiques et littéraires*, Paris, 1875. 2 vols.

Lehugeur, P., *Histoire de Philippe le Long 1316-1322*, Paris, 1897.

Le Roux de Lincy and L. Tisserand, *Paris et ses historiens*, Paris, 1867.

Levis-Mirepoix, A. de, *Philippe-le-Bel*, Paris, 1936.

Liebman, C., *Etude sur la vie en prose de Saint Denis*, New York, Geneva, 1942.

MacKinney, L., "Double-pestle Action in Medieval Miniatures," *American Pharmaceutical Association Journal*, n.s. 1, 1961, 161, 162.

————. *Medical Illustrations in Medieval Manuscripts*, London, 1965.

Martin, H., *Légende de Saint Denis*, Paris, 1908.

————. *Les Joyaux de l'enluminure à la bibliothèque nationale*, Paris, 1928.

————. *La Miniature française du XIIIe au XVe siècle*, Paris, 1923.

Le Ménagier de Paris: traité de morale et d'économie domestique composé vers 1393 par un bourgeois parisien, Paris, 1846. 2 vols.

Michaëlsson, K., "Le Livre de la taille de Paris, l'an de grace 1313," *Göteborgs högskolas årsskrift*, LVII, 1951, no. 3, 1-349.

————. "Le Livre de la taille de Paris l'an 1296," *Göteborgs universitets årsskrift*, LXIV, 1958, no. 4, 1-308.

————. "Le Livre de la taille de Paris l'an 1297," *Göteborgs universitets årsskrift*, LXVII, 1961, no. 3, 1-480.

Millar, E., *An Illuminated Manuscript of La Somme le Roy Attributed to the Parisian Miniaturist Honoré*, Oxford, 1953.

—————. *The Parisian Miniaturist Honoré*, London, 1959.

Morand, K., *Jean Pucelle*, Oxford, 1962.

—————. *Jean Pucelle and His Workshop*, unpublished Ph.D. dissertation, London, University of London, 1958.

The National Gallery of Canada, *Art and the Courts, France and England from 1259-1328*, Ottawa, 1972. 2 vols.

The New Palaeographical Society, Facsimiles of Ancient Manuscripts, ed. E. M. Thompson, G. F. Warner, F. G. Kenyon, J. P. Gilson, London, 1st ser., 1903-1912, II, pls. 88-90.

Newton, A., *Travel and Travellers in the Middle Ages*, London, 1949.

Nordenfalk, C., "Französische Buchmalerei 1200-1500," *Kunst-Chronik*, IX, 1956, 179-189.

—————. "Maître Honoré et Mâitre Pucelle," *Apollo*, LXXIX, 1964, 358-364.

Olschki, L., *Paris nach den altfranzösischen nationalen Epen. Topographie, Stadtgeschichte und lokale Sagen*, Heidelberg, 1913.

Ordonnances des roys de France . . . , Paris, 1723-1849. vols. I and XII especially.

Panofsky, E., *Early Netherlandish Painting*, Cambridge (Mass.), 1953. 2 vols.

Paris. Bibliothèque impériale, département des manuscrits, *Catalogue des manuscrits français*, Paris, 1868-1902. 5 vols.

—————. Bibliothèque nationale, *La Librairie de Charles V*, Paris, 1968.

—————. —————. *Les Manuscrits à peintures en France du XIIIe au XVIe siècle*, Paris, 1955.

Piton, C., *Le Costume civil en France du XIIIe au XIXe siècle*, Paris, 1926.

Porcher, J., *Medieval French Miniatures*, New York, 1959.

Power, E. (trans.), *The Goodman of Paris (le ménagier de Paris); A Treatise on Moral and Domestic Economy by a Citizen of Paris (c. 1393)*, London, 1928.

Prost, B., "Liste des artistes mentionnés dans les états de la maison du roi et des maisons des princes, du XIIIe siècle à l'an 1500," *Archives historiques, artistiques et littéraires*, I, 1889-1890, 425-437.

Quatrebarbes, T., *Oeuvres complètes du roi René . . .* , Angers, 1843-1846. 4 vols. in 2.

Quicherat, J., "Le Commerce et les métiers de Paris au moyen âge," *Magasin pittoresque*, XIV, 1846, 217-222.

Raynaud, G. and H. Lemaitre (eds.), *Le Roman de Renart le Contrefait*, Paris, 1914. 2 vols.

Réau, L., *Histoire de la peinture au moyen âge: la miniature*, Melun, 1946.

Recueil des historiens des Gaules et de la France, Paris, 1840-1904. 24 vols.

Reinach, S., " 'Sainte Geneviève sur Notre-Dame de Paris,' Miniature parisienne du XVe siècle," *Gazette des beaux arts*, LXIV, 1922, pt. 2, 257-264.

Renart, J., *Galeran de Bretagne*, ed. L. Foulet, Paris, 1925.

Richard, J.-M., *Une Petite-Nièce de Saint Louis Mahaut comtesse d'Artois et de Bourgogne*, Paris, 1887.

Saulnier, V.-L., *La Littérature française du moyen âge des origines à 1500*, Paris, 1948.

Sauval, H., *L'Histoire et recherches des antiquités de la ville de Paris*, Paris, 1724. 3 vols.

Le Siècle de Saint Louis, Paris, 1970.

Staley, E., *King René d'Anjou and His Seven Queens*, New York, 1912.

Tarr, L., *The History of the Carriage*, New York, 1969.

Thévenot, M., *Catalogue des manuscrits de la bibliothèque de défunt monseigneur le chancelier Séguier*, Paris, 1686.

Tolnay, C. de, "The Music of the Universe," *The Journal of the Walters Art Gallery*, VI, 1943, 90, 93; fig. 11.

Valois, N., "Jean de Jandun et Marsile de Padoue, auteurs du *Defensor pacis*," *Histoire littéraire de la France*, XXXIII, 1906, 528-623.

Vernet, A., "L'Inondation de 1296-1297 à Paris," *Mémoires de la fédération des sociétés historiques et archéologiques de Paris et de l'Ile-de-France*, I, 1949, 47-56.

Viard, J. (ed.), *Journaux du trésor de Philippe IV le Bel*, Paris, 1940.

Viellard, J., *Le Guide du pèlerin de Saint-Jacques de Compostelle. Texte latin du XIIe siècle édité et traduit en français d'après les manuscrits de Compostelle et de Ripoll*, Macon, 1950.

Eugène Viollet le Duc 1814-1879, Paris, 1965.

Viollet-le-Duc, E., *Dictionnaire raisonné de l'architecture française du XIe au XVIe siècle*, Paris, 1858-1868. 10 vols.

Vitzthum von Eckstädt, G., *Die Pariser Miniaturmalerei von der Zeit des hl. Ludwig bis zu Philipp von Valois und ihr Verhältnis zur Malerei in Nordwesteuropa*, Leipzig, 1907.

Vollmöller, K., *Octavian*, Heilbronn, 1883.

White, T. H., *The Bestiary, A Book of Beasts*, New York, 1960.

LIBRARY OF CONGRESS CATALOGING IN PUBLICATION DATA

Egbert, Virginia Wylie.
    On the bridges of mediaeval Paris.

    Bibliography: p.
    1. Paris—Bridges.   2. Paris—Social life and
customs—Pictorial works.   3. Paris.   Bibliothèque
nationale.   MSS.   (Fr. 2090-2092)   I. Title.
DC761.E35   914.4′36   74-2964
ISBN 0-691-03906-2